Great American Writers

TWENTIETH CENTURY

EDITOR
R. BAIRD SHUMAN
University of Illinois

Stephen Vincent Benét • Judy Blume
Arna Bontemps • Gwendolyn Brooks • Pearl S. Buck
Truman Capote • Raymond Carver • Willa Cather

MARSHALL CAVENDISH
NEW YORK • TORONTO • LONDON • SYDNEY

Marshall Cavendish
99 White Plains Road
Tarrytown, New York 10591-9001

Website: www.marshallcavendish.com

© 2002 Marshall Cavendish Corporation

Salem Press

Editor: R. Baird Shuman
Managing Editor: R. Kent Rasmussen

Manuscript Editors: Heather Stratton
Lauren M. Mitchell
Assistant Editor: Andrea Miller
Research Supervisor: Jeffry Jensen
Acquisitions Editor: Mark Rehn

Marshall Cavendish

Project Editor: Marian Armstrong
Editorial Director: Paul Bernabeo

Designer: Patrice Sheridan

Photo Research: Candlepants
Carousel Research
Linda Sykes Picture Research
Anne Burns Images

Indexing: AEIOU

Library of Congress Cataloging-in-Publication Data

Great American writers: twentieth century / R. Baird Shuman, editor.
    v. cm.
    Includes bibliographical references and indexes.
    Contents: v. 1. Agee-Bellow--v. 2. Benét-Cather--v. 3. Cormier-Dylan--v. 4. Eliot-Frost--v. 5. Gaines-Hinton--v. 6. Hughes-Lewis--v. 7. London-McNickle--v. 8. Miller-O'Connor--v. 9. O'Neill-Rich--v. 10. Salinger-Stein--v. 11. Steinbeck-Walker--v. 12. Welty-Zindel--v. 13. Index.
    ISBN 0-7614-7240-1 (set)—ISBN 0-7614-7242-8 (v. 2)
    1. American literature--20th century--Bio-bibliography--Dictionaries.
    2. Authors, American--20th century--Biography--Dictionaries. 3. American literature--20th century--Dictionaries. I. Shuman, R. Baird (Robert Baird), 1929-

PS221.G74 2002
810.9'005'03
[B]   2001028461

Printed in Malaysia; bound in the United States

07 06 05 04 03 02   6 5 4 3 2 1

Contents

Stephen Vincent Benét

BORN: July 22, 1898, Bethlehem, Pennsylvania
DIED: March 13, 1943, New York, New York
IDENTIFICATION: Early twentieth-century American poet, novelist, and short-story writer, best known for his poetry and other writings about popular subjects taken from American history and folklore.

During the 1930s and 1940s Stephen Vincent Benét was one of the best-known and most widely read American poets, respected by critical reviewers and honored in poetry workshops and university lecture halls. His work celebrates American legends, myths, and folklore and is significant for its historical accuracy and patriotism. *John Brown's Body* (1928), his long narrative poem about the U.S. Civil War, was acclaimed as an American epic and quickly made him a national celebrity. Although Benét's novels were less notable than his poetry, some of his short stories met with success. He was awarded a Pulitzer Prize for *John Brown's Body* in 1929 and another, posthumously, for *Western Star* (1943). *John Brown's Body* and collections of Benét's better-known stories have remained uninterruptedly in print.

The Writer's Life

Stephen Vincent Benét was born on July 22, 1898, in Bethlehem, Pennsylvania, the son of James Walker and Frances Neill (Rose) Benét. His father served as a career artillery officer in the U.S. Army. Stephen's grandfather and namesake, Brigadier General Stephen Vincent Benét, had also been an artillery officer in the U.S. Army from 1874 to 1891.

Benét's family was literary as well as military. His father loved poetry, and his mother enjoyed reading and writing. His older brother, William Rose Benét, and older sister, Laura Amanda (Benét) Walker, both became poets and writers of considerable stature.

Benét seated and writing, date unknown. Although Benét wrote in many genres, he is best known for his poetry, for which he received two Pulitzer Prizes, one posthumously.

Childhood. As a child, Benét moved with his family to a series of Army bases from Pennsylvania to California and later to Georgia. At the age of three he contracted scarlet fever, and the disease impaired his eyesight and his general health through the rest of his life. Until the age of twelve, he was educated at home through correspondence lessons. At twelve, Benét entered the Hitchcock Military Academy in Jacinto, California.

After moving to his father's new command post in Augusta, Georgia, Benét attended Summerville Academy from 1911 to 1915. It was a pleasant experience for him. He excelled in school and had plenty of time to read his favorite authors, including William Makepeace Thackeray, Rudyard Kipling, and G. K. Chesterton.

The Young Writer. When he was thirteen, Benét won a special cash prize from the St. Nicholas League for a poem he had written. One year later, his ballad about Robin Hood, "A Song of the Woods" (1912), won the league's silver badge and was published in *St. Nicholas Magazine*. In 1914 another of his poems won the league's gold badge. Before he was seventeen, Benét had sold his first poem to *The New Republic*. In 1915 he published his first book of poetry, *Five Men and Pompey,* a series of classical dramatic monologues.

College Years. At the age of seventeen, Benét entered Yale University. Although he was a mediocre student, he found time to read poetry and American history and served on the editorial staffs of many Yale student publications. Benét won a number of literary prizes at Yale, including three John Masefield poetry awards and two Albert Stanburrough Cook Awards. His *Young Adventure: A Book of Poems* was published in the Yale Series of Younger Poets in 1918.

After graduating from Yale in 1919, Benét worked briefly as an advertising copywriter in New York City, but he returned to graduate school at Yale the following year. In 1920 he earned a master of arts degree. His master's thesis was a group of poems that were published under the title *Heavens and Earth* (1920), for which he shared the Poetry Society of America Award with Carl Sandburg in 1921.

Marriage and Children. Upon receiving a traveling fellowship from Yale in the summer of 1920, Benét went to Paris to study at the Sorbonne and work on his poetry and fiction. While there, he met Rosemary Carr, and they were married when they returned to the United States in 1921. They were happily married for the remainder of Benét's life and had three children: Stephanie Jane, Thomas Carr, and Rachel Felicity. Stephen and Rosemary both loved poetry, and they collaborated to write *A Book of Americans* (1933), a series of poems for children about famous American people.

Struggles and Accomplishments. Benét's first novel, *The Beginning of Wisdom* (1921), was soon followed by two more, *Young People's Pride* (1922) and *Jean Huguenot* (1923). More important to his future success, however, were three poems, "The Ballad of William Sycamore" (1922), "King David" (1923), and "The Mountain Whippoorwill" (1925). Unfortunately, neither his novels nor early poetry successes brought him much financial security. In order to support his family, he spent much time reviewing books and plays and writing formula short stories for magazines. In 1926 he completed his fourth novel, *Spanish Bayonet.*

In 1926 Benét was awarded a Guggenheim Memorial fellowship of $2,500 to write a long poem on an American subject. He went to Paris to work on the project. After eighteen months, he completed *John Brown's Body,* an epic poem about the U.S. Civil War. Published in 1928, it was an immediate critical and popular success. Benét quickly became the best-known living poet in the United States. He was awarded a Pulitzer Prize for *John Brown's Body* in 1929. Between 1928 and 1929, the poem earned him about $25,000 in royalties—a vast sum at that time.

Success in the 1930s. Benét wrote some of his most successful short stories in the 1930s, including "The Devil and Daniel Webster" (1937), "Johnny Pye and the Fool-Killer" (1937), and "Doc Mellhorn and the Pearly Gates" (1938). In 1932 he was awarded an O. Henry Memorial Prize for the best American short story of the year, "An End to Dreams." During the 1930s, Benét lectured widely and advised publishing houses and younger writers. In 1938 he was elected to the American Academy of Arts and Letters. Motivated by the

Horace Pippin's 1942 oil painting *John Brown Going to His Hanging* (The Pennsylvania Academy of the Fine Arts) depicts the final moments of the abolitionist's life. While never idolizing Brown, Benét clearly states the significance of Brown's life and the hope and inspiration his memory evokes in his epic poem *John Brown's Body.*

HIGHLIGHTS IN BENÉT'S LIFE

1898	Stephen Vincent Benét is born on July 22 in Bethlehem, Pennsylvania.
1911–1915	Attends Summerville Academy in Augusta, Georgia.
1915	Publishes first book of poetry, *Five Men and Pompey*.
1919	Awarded bachelor's degree from Yale University.
1920	Earns master's degree from Yale.
1920–1921	Studies at the Sorbonne in Paris; publishes first novel, *The Beginning of Wisdom*; marries Rosemary Carr.
1924	First child, Stephanie, is born.
1926	Benét wins a Guggenheim Fellowship; son, Thomas Carr, is born.
1928	Publishes his most successful work, *John Brown's Body*, for which he receives a Pulitzer Prize.
1931	Last child, Rachel, is born.
1932	Benét receives O. Henry Memorial Prize for "An End to Dreams."
1933	Receives Roosevelt Medal for his contribution to American letters.
1937	Publishes his most successful short story, "The Devil and Daniel Webster," which wins an O. Henry Memorial Prize.
1940	Receives O. Henry Memorial Prize for "Freedom's Hard-Bought Thing."
1943	Dies in New York City on March 13.
1944	Awarded a posthumous Pulitzer Prize for *Western Star*.
1998	U.S. Postal Service issues a Benét commemorative stamp.

Great Depression and the Nazi movement in Europe, Benét for the first time in his career began to write poetry and fiction with an angry political edge. Many of these writings were published in his book *Burning City* (1936).

The Final Years. In the late 1930s Benét's health steadily declined. He suffered devastating attacks of arthritis of the spine. In 1939 he was hospitalized for several weeks with nervous exhaustion. With the entry of the United States into World War II in 1941, Benét set his professional writing career aside and devoted himself to writing articles for the Office of War Information, the Writers' War Board, and the Council for Democracy. He also wrote scripts for the radio series *Dear Adolf* and *This Is War*. In 1943 he wrote a short history of the United States, titled *America* (1944), for distribution throughout the world.

Overwhelmed by a heavy schedule of writing and public appearances, Benét died of a heart attack at his home in New York City on March 13, 1943. The following year, he was posthumously awarded another Pulitzer Prize for *Western Star*.

The Writer's Work

Stephen Vincent Benét wrote poetry, long and short fiction, nonfiction, plays, and screenplays. He is best known for his poetry, which he wrote in great abundance and with remarkable success. His poems and short stories on popular topics from U.S. history and folklore have been widely read, studied, anthologized, and adapted to the stage and screen. The majority of Benét's work celebrates the United States' past in a style based on oral folktales and folk ballads.

Issues in Benét's Poetry and Fiction.

The inspiration of the United States's past, which was deeply rooted in Benét's childhood, is the predominant characteristic in all of his work. Benét embraced U.S. history and was preoccupied with historical themes that included a spectrum of the people and races that constitute the United States. He invented stories dealing with people from across the country.

Although the majority of Benét's American literary contemporaries evinced a deep sense of pessimism about society and civilization following World War I, Benét reached into the United States's past to find optimism and conviction about the future. In portraying a United States that had real vitality, Benét's writings contain a balanced blend of humor, affection, originality, imagination, and technical skill. His topics involve U.S. society, history, politics, and the supernatural.

People in Benét's Writings.

Benét wrote about prominent historical figures such as Abraham Lincoln and Robert E. Lee in *John*

FILMS BASED ON BENÉT'S WORKS

Year	Title
1925	The Necessary Evil
1930	Abraham Lincoln
1938	Love, Honor, and Behave
1939	The Devil and Daniel Webster (opera)
1941	Cheers for Miss Bishop
1941	All That Money Can Buy
1954	Seven Brides for Seven Brothers

George Caleb Bingham's 1852 oil painting *Daniel Boone Escorting Settlers Through the Cumberland Gap* portrays the famous American pioneer guiding a group of unknown settlers. Well-known historical figures such as Boone, as well as everyday Americans from all walks of life, are skillfully woven into Benét's stories and poems.

Brown's Body, but he also depicted a wide variety of common Americans of many backgrounds, occupations, and opinions. In *John Brown's Body,* Benét masterfully portrayed the views of both his Southern and his Northern Civil War-era characters, from Southern aristocrats and their slaves to farm boys and soldiers from New England. In *A Book of Americans* (1933), Benét and his wife brought many historical Americans, including Thomas Jefferson, Daniel Boone, Jesse James, and John James Audubon, to life in a series of lighthearted poems.

Later Themes in Benét's Writings. A number of critical developments in the 1930s, particularly the Great Depression, the rise of fascism in Europe, and the emergence of demagogues such as Father Charles E. Coughlin in the United States, took Benét in a different direction with his writing. He wrote several poems that expressed apocalyptic visions of social collapse, including "Metropolitan Nightmare" (1933), "Litany of Dictatorships" (1935), "Ode to the Austrian Socialists" (1936), and "Nightmare at Noon" (1940). Likewise, numerous short stories, particularly "Silver Jemmy" (1936), "The

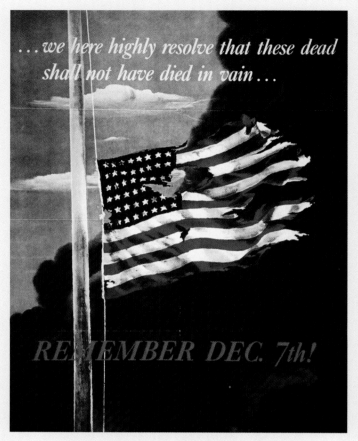

...we here highly resolve that these dead shall not have died in vain...

REMEMBER DEC. 7th!

The words on this 1941 World War II poster commemorating the attack on Pearl Harbor express a powerful sense of patriotism, a theme that permeates much of Benét's work. Benét, a strong and optimistic voice throughout World War II, set aside his own professional career to write articles related to the war.

SOME INSPIRATIONS BEHIND BENÉT'S WORK

Much of Benét's motivation to become a writer, and particularly a poet, resulted from his parents' love for poetry. His father loved to read, recite, and discuss poetry. In addition, his mother was an avid reader of, and occasional writer of, poetry. Benét was also influenced to pursue a writing career by his brother and sister, both of whom became respected poets and writers. As a youth, Benét read extensively about American military history, which prepared him for his later works on American subjects.

While attending Yale University, Benét's English professor, Henry Seidel, encouraged Benét to write in numerous literary genres. Benét's writing efforts were also influenced and encouraged by many of his undergraduate friends at Yale, particularly Philip Barry, Archibald MacLeish, and Thornton Wilder, all of whom later distinguished themselves in literature.

POETRY

1915   Five Men and Pompey
1918   Young Adventure: A
       Book of Poems
1920   Heavens and Earth
1923   King David
1925   Tiger Joy
1928   John Brown's Body
1931   Ballads and Poems,
       1915–1930
1933   A Book of Americans
       (with Rosemary Carr
       Benét)
1936   Burning City
1939   The Ballad of the Duke's
       Mercy
1943   Western Star

LONG FICTION

1921   The Beginning of
       Wisdom
1922   Young People's Pride
1923   Jean Huguenot
1926   Spanish Bayonet
1934   James Shore's Daughter

SHORT FICTION

1930   The Litter of Rose
       Leaves
1937   Thirteen O'Clock
1938   Johnny Pye and the
       Fool-Killer
1939   Tales Before Midnight
1943   Twenty-five Short Stories

PLAYS

1924   Nerves (with John
       Chipman Farrar)
1924   That Awful Mrs. Eaton
       (with Farrar)
1937   The Headless Horseman
       (previously published)
1938   The Devil and Daniel
       Webster
1942   A Child Is Born: A
       Modern Drama of the
       Nativity

RADIO PLAYS

1945   We Stand United, and
       Other Radio Scripts

SCREENPLAYS

1930   Abraham Lincoln
1941   Cheers for Miss Bishop
1941   All That Money Can Buy

NONFICTION

1941   Listen to the People
1944   America
1946   Stephen Vincent Benét
       on Writing: A Great
       Writer's Letters of
       Advice to a Young
       Beginner
1960   Selected Letters of
       Stephen Vincent Benét

COLLECTIONS

1942   Selected Works of
       Stephen Vincent Benét,
       ed. Basil Davenport
1946   The Last Circle: Stories
       and Poems
1942   Stephen Vincent Benét:
       Selected Poetry and
       Prose, ed. Basil
       Davenport

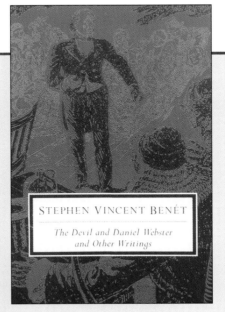

STEPHEN VINCENT BENÉT
*The Devil and Daniel Webster
and Other Writings*

Blood of Martyrs" (1936), and "Into Egypt" (1939), expressed similar fears and concerns.

In the early 1940s, Benét was a strong advocate of the United States' entry into World War II. During this time, his writing reflected a strong voice for patriotism and national optimism. To help ensure U.S. survival during World War II, he devoted his time and energy to patriotic writings, such as "We Stand United" (1940), "A Summons to Be Free" (1941), "Listen to the People" (1941), and *America* (1944).

Benét's Literary Legacy.
Benét's name fits well with those of F. Scott Fitzgerald and Ernest Hemingway as one of the American writers who came to prominence between World War I and World War II. Benét's poems are remarkable in their imaginative evocation of the American scene. His short stories display a feeling for American folklore and legend, a skilled use of grotesque and supernatural themes, and a talent for unusual ideas and effects. In his poetry, novels, and short fiction, Benét demonstrated a gift for

clear, rapid narration and an ability to bring scenes vividly to life with image and metaphor. For his poems and best stories on traditional American subjects, Benét has earned a reputation as an author who gave artistic form to his profound love and vast knowledge of his country. Ultimately, Benét may well be remembered as a talented writer comparable to Henry Wadsworth Longfellow, Carl Sandburg, and Vachel Lindsay.

BIBLIOGRAPHY

Benét, Laura. *When William Rose, Stephen Vincent, and I Were Young.* New York: Dodd, Mead, 1976.

Benét, William Rose. *Stephen Vincent Benét: My Brother Steve.* 1943. Reprint. New York: Farrar & Rinehart, 1977.

Brenner, Rica. *Poets of Our Time.* New York: Harcourt, Brace, 1941.

Capps, Jack L., and C. Robert Kemble. Introduction and Notes to *John Brown's Body.* New York: Holt, Rinehart and Winston, 1968.

Deutsch, Babette. *Poetry in Our Time.* New York: Holt, 1952.

Fenton, Charles A. *Stephen Vincent Benét: The Life and Times of an American Man of Letters, 1898–1943.* 1958. Reprint. New Haven, Conn.: Yale University Press, 1978.

_____, ed. *Selected Letters of Stephen Vincent Benét.* New Haven, Conn.: Yale University Press, 1960.

Gregory, Horace, and Mary Zaturenska. *A History of American Poetry, 1900–1940.* New York: Harcourt, Brace, 1946.

Kunitz, Stanley J., and Howard Haycraft, eds. *Twentieth Century Authors.* New York: H. W. Wilson, 1961.

Stroud, Perry Edmund. *Stephen Vincent Benét.* New York: Twayne Publishers, 1962.

The nineteenth-century painting *The New Frontier* (artist unknown) reflects the vastness of the lands and mountains of the American Frontier. Much of Benét's writing concentrates on the opening of the West and the adaptations of generations as they settled America.

Reader's Guide to Major Works

"THE DEVIL AND DANIEL WEBSTER"

Genre: Short story
Subgenre: Moral conflict
Published: New York, 1937
Time period: Nineteenth century
Setting: New England

Themes and Issues. "The Devil and Daniel Webster" is delightful, entertaining literature that glorifies the American ideals of freedom and human dignity, thus capturing the American dream. It is based on an old German legend about a magician named Faust who sold his soul to the devil in return for temporary gain. A great deal of U.S. history is woven into the story, including the career, personality, family, and great speeches of the New England lawyer and politician Daniel Webster (1782–1852); the background of the Civil War; famous and infamous men who played a part in the American past, including Webster, Walter Butler, Simon Girty, King Philip, Teach the Pirate, Governor Dale, Benedict Arnold, Reverend John Smeet, and Judge Hathorne of the Salem witchcraft trials.

The story eulogizes Daniel Webster, who emerges from the pages of history as a vivid American folk hero: courageous, dynamic, idealistic, and bigger than life. Webster eloquently addresses such important issues as the ideals of freedom, dignity, integrity, and the glory of humankind. A persuasive appeal to idealism is Webster's approach to combating hostility and winning arguments and debates.

The Plot. Poor New Hampshire farmer Jabez Stone is in financial straits, about to lose his farm to foreclosure. Uttering aloud that he would sell his soul to the devil for two cents, Jabez receives a visit from Mr. Scratch, the devil. After he strikes a deal with Mr. Scratch, Jabez enjoys a decade of prosperity. He grows increasingly greedy and cruel as time progresses, but he still has a lot of good in him.

When Mr. Scratch eventually arrives at Jabez's wedding to claim his soul, Jabez appeals to his houseguest, Daniel Webster, to defend him. The great American statesman and orator agrees to help Jabez and gives a stirring oration at midnight before a wicked judge and jury of historical American villains selected by the devil. Webster's eloquent and diplomatic tactics win an acquittal for Jabez. Webster even lets the devil go free.

Analysis. In many ways, "The Devil and Daniel Webster" is an American analogy of the biblical story of Job, in which Job questions why the righteous suffer, and the legend of Faust. Benét combines a superlative story with several thematic elements and a wide range of tone, from broad Yankee humor to even nobility, to form a classic American fable. Virtually every sentence of the story is cleverly written, making it an example of literature at its entertaining best. However, the story is also very rich with wholesome meaning, with a moral at its center.

Near the end of the story, Webster's oration on the ideals of freedom and human dignity contains some of Benét's finest passages. Webster miraculously obtains mercy from the stone-hearted judge and jury by recounting the failures of all men and pointing out that the things that are good for any man can only be enjoyed under freedom.

SOURCES FOR FURTHER STUDY

Clark, Bruce B., and Robert K. Thomas. *Out of the Best Books.* Vol. 5. Salt Lake City, Utah: Deseret, 1970.

Fenton, Charles A. *Stephen Vincent Benét: The Life and Times of an American Man of Letters, 1898–1943.* New Haven, Conn.: Yale University Press, 1958.

Ludington, Townsend, ed. *"The Devil and Daniel Webster" and Other Writings.* New York: Viking Penguin, 1999.

Stroud, Perry Edmund. *Stephen Vincent Benét.* New York: Twayne Publishers, 1962.

John Brown is the central figure in this section of John Steuart Curry's mural *Tragic Prelude*, which Curry painted on the walls of the Capitol Building in Topeka, Kansas, from 1937 to 1942. Curry's own words about the mural were, "In this group is expressed the fratricidal fury that first flamed on the plains of Kansas, the tragic prelude to the last bloody feud of the English-speaking people."

JOHN BROWN'S BODY

Genre: Poetry
Subgenre: Epic narrative
Published: New York, 1928
Time period: 1859–1865
Setting: United States

Themes and Issues. *John Brown's Body* spans some of the most critical years in the history of the United States, from abolitionist John Brown's raid on the federal arsenal in Harpers Ferry, Virginia, in October, 1859, through the Civil War, to Confederate general Robert E. Lee's surrender on April 9, 1865, at Appomattox Courthouse, Virginia. The poem is not intended to be a eulogy of Brown, whose faults are clearly shown, but an epic narrative illustrating the diversity upon which the United States has been built. This work is the boldest attempt in literature to treat American history poetically.

The focus shifts from federal government cabinet officers to frontiersmen and from Civil War battle scenes to domestic events.

Many of the people described were real people who played an important part in U.S. history, including Abraham Lincoln, Robert E. Lee, Jefferson Davis, and Ulysses S. Grant. Others are fictional characters representing ordinary men and women who lived through war and peace and faced many of the same problems that people face today. The fates of these characters reflect Benét's interpretation of the human complexities of the Civil War. The modern United States is built upon their decisions and the outcome of the war.

The Plot. John Brown's attempt to free the slaves by raiding Harpers Ferry in 1859, the associated expression of public opinion, and Brown's trial and execution constitutes the majority of book 1. Later, in books 4 and 5, Brown is reprimanded for his actions. In the final book of the poem, book 8, the historical significance of Brown's raid and life are summed up, and lessons are derived from Brown's character and actions. After the

Confederate victory at the Second Battle of Manassas, Union hopes were at their lowest, and Brown's spirit was invoked by editors and preachers to buoy up the North. Subsequently, President Lincoln issued the Emancipation Proclamation, freeing all slaves in recaptured rebel territories.

Much of the poem follows the adventures of the primary fictional characters who represent the main regional divisions of the United States: Jack Ellyat, a Northern soldier from Connecticut; Clay Wingate, a Southern soldier from Georgia; and Melora Vilas and her father John, who live on a farm in Tennessee and typify the border states and the West. The fates of these characters and of minor figures in the poem are resolved by the events of the Civil War.

In a battle near Pittsburg Landing, Tennessee, Ellyat flees the battle in fear for his life, winding up at the Vilas farm. He and Melora fall in love, and she becomes pregnant. When Jack is captured by the South, he and Melora are separated until the end of the war. As the events of the Civil War unfold, Melora and her father travel from place to place searching for Jack. Eventually, Melora finds Jack, and they later marry.

Meanwhile, Clay Wingate returns to Georgia on a leave from the Confederate army and begins a new romance with Lucy Weatherby, a coquettish Virginian whose sweetheart was killed at the Battle of Bull Run. For a period of time, she replaces Wingate's former love, Sally Dupre. After returning to war, Wingate is wounded in a skirmish in Virginia. In the meantime, his home in Georgia, Wingate Hall, accidentally burns to the ground. After the war, when Clay returns to Georgia, Sally is waiting for him and they marry.

Analysis. Over three hundred pages and nearly fifteen thousand lines long, *John Brown's Body* ranks with the great epics of Western literature. Benét captures events of the Civil War in verse that is graceful, accessible, and sometimes stirring. As he himself suggests, the poem is a "cyclorama" of shifting times, places, and viewpoints, with the reader at the center of the action. Critics have both praised and scorned the poem. Some commentators claim that Benét's characterizations of President Lincoln and General Lee are shallow and inept, while others judge them as insightful and faithful to the real people. Benét's choice of a wide range of poetic meters to portray different characters results in stylistic looseness and fragmentation, meaning that the poem must be studied in separate, individual sections, rather than as a whole.

The unifying element of the poem is the spirit of John Brown. Benét regards Brown as an important instrument and symbol in U.S. history. After Brown's hanging, his memory gives hope and inspiration to the North through the dismal early days of the Civil War. Benét's selection of fictional characters represents all of the regions and social groups of the United States at the time. By tracing the fortunes of such a diverse group of people, Benét illustrates how the war affects them, and how they affect the growth and development of a nation. Benét is admired for his accurate, sympathetic treatment of both Northern and Southern characters. The struggles, failures, and successes of Ellyat, Wingate, Vilas, and Dupre are representations of those encountered by humankind throughout history.

SOURCES FOR FURTHER STUDY

Capps, Jack L., and C. Robert Kemble. Introduction and Notes to *John Brown's Body*. New York: Holt, Rinehart and Winston, 1968.

Fenton, Charles A. *Stephen Vincent Benét: The Life and Times of an American Man of Letters, 1898–1943*. New Haven, Conn.: Yale University Press, 1958.

Gregory, Horace, and Mary Zaturenska. *A History of American Poetry, 1900–1940*. New York: Harcourt, Brace, 1946.

Stroud, Perry Edmund. *Stephen Vincent Benét*. New York: Twayne Publishers, 1962.

Other Works

"THE BALLAD OF WILLIAM SYCAMORE, 1790–1871" (1922). This poem is often selected by anthology editors as Stephen Vincent Benét's best representation of lyrical Americanism. Benét sums up the life of a representative frontiersman, William Sycamore, with exact rhymes, precision ballad meter, and clarity. The invigorating life of the western frontier is captured in a succession of American images. Many of the images are associated with birth or death, such as the sons sowed like apple seeds on the wagon trails and the green fir that serves as the mother's doctor.

William Sycamore's birth on twigs of pine plays upon the evergreen symbol of immortality. He is one of the innumerable literary sons of James Fenimore Cooper's Natty Bumppo who fled westward from the spreading American civilization. The poem is intimately linked with the many American legends of the frontier. The peaceful immortality that William Sycamore enjoys at the end moves the poem deeper into the realm of myth. Rooted deeply in American history, this ballad illustrates the desire to be at one with nature's wild, untouched beauty.

"JACOB AND THE INDIANS" (1938). Benét sounds an emphatic message of faith in "Jacob and the Indians." A shy young scholar, Jacob Stein, goes through the ordeal of learning to believe in himself. As he gradually matures, he begins to see himself not only as a person with unexpected strengths and continuing weaknesses but also as a part of something bigger than self.

Jacob's developing faith in America cannot be separated from his growing belief in himself and the people who test him. His first companion on the frontier, McCampbell, is a Calvinist whose religious convictions are diametrically opposed to Jacob's Jewish teachings. McCampbell is obsessed with the idea that the Indians beyond the western mountains are the Lost Tribes of Israel. Jacob learns much from McCampbell, particularly about tolerance. After McCampbell's death, another Gentile, Raphael Sanchez, becomes Jacob's partner. The final words that Jacob shares with Raphael are that the country he has seen must be made available to everyone.

By the time that Jacob returns to

The pine symbolizes the immortality of the title character in Benét's poem "The Ballad of William Sycamore" as well as the endurance of the American legacy.

The vulnerability of a small craft exposed to the hazards of the open sea in James Abbot McNeil Whistler's oil painting *The Sea* reflects the helplessness of Andrew Beard, the main character in Benét's novel *The Spanish Bayonet*, as he witnesses the shooting death of his lady love at sea.

Philadelphia, his vision of himself and others has grown to match the vastness of the lands and mountains that he has seen and crossed. This story successfully weaves the staple American themes of tolerance, trade, the opening of the West, and the transformation of characters in the settlement of America. "Jacob and the Indians" portrays Benét's recurring theme of the reality of the American dream, and incorporates much American history into a short story.

SPANISH BAYONET (1926). Often regarded as Benét's best novel, *Spanish Bayonet* is a historical romance and adventure set on the Spanish island of Minorca a decade before the American Revolution and in Florida a decade after it. Andrew Beard, the younger son of a wealthy New York Tory merchant, is sent by his father to a colony in Florida to evaluate its structure, methods, products, and loyalty to the Crown. Andrew eventually becomes involved with the lovely Sparta Gentian, daughter of the colony's founder. After their marriage, Andrew makes the shocking discovery that Sparta is another man's mistress and has an un-

quenchable thirst for power. Imprisoned for attempting to murder Sparta's father, Andrew eventually escapes and leaves Florida with his new love, Caterina. However, as they are fleeing in a small boat, Caterina is shot and dies. A bereft Andrew returns to New York and joins the revolutionary forces during the American Revolution.

The story follows Andrew from relative innocence to young adulthood, where he gains an awareness of the evils of the world and the responsibilities of life. As he becomes enlightened about the real world, Andrew is disappointed to find it much different than he had imagined, but he faces up to it. The bush of Spanish bayonet flowers that Andrew first encountered on his arrival in Florida becomes the symbol of the implicit danger in Andrew's life. The white petals rising from the green spikes of the Spanish bayonet also symbolize the whole concept of romance, an intriguing jeopardy that reality makes remote. *Spanish Bayonet* is limited in its objectives, unified in theme and structure, and consistent in the mode and quality of its style.

 *Resources*

Most of the manuscripts and correspondence of Stephen Vincent Benét can be found at Yale University in the Yale Collection of American Literature and in the manuscript collections of Cornell University.

Audio Tapes. Benét's work was often heard on the radio in the early 1940s. Some of these programs were re-broadcast in 1998 through a special arrangement with the National Broadcasting Corporation. "Listen to the People" features the voice of Ethel Barrymore. "They Burned the Books" stars Paul Muni. Excerpts from *John Brown's Body* feature Tyrone Power, Judith Anderson, and Raymond Massey. (http://www.wvia.org/fm/programs/benet.html)

Commemorative Stamp. A U.S. postage stamp that salutes both Benét's great writing talent and the heroism and tragedy that marked the Civil War was issued on July 22, 1998 at Harpers Ferry, West Virginia. This stamp is the fifteenth in the Literary Arts series. (http://www.stampsonline.com/collect/stamp98/benetleft.html)

State Marker. A Pennsylvania marker honoring Benét is located near Bethlehem, Pennsylvania, at Fountain Hill on the corner of Ostrum and Bishop Thorpe Streets.

Television Documentary. Lehigh Valley public television station in Lehigh Valley, Pennsylvania, and the Stephen Vincent Benét Centennial Committee produced an inspiring story about Benét titled "Out of American Earth: The Story of Stephen Vincent Benét," which was originally broadcast on July 22, 1998. (http://www.lehighvalleypbs.org/aboutlvpbs/PressReleases/Benet.html)

ALVIN K. BENSON

Judy Blume

BORN: February 12, 1938, Elizabeth, New Jersey
IDENTIFICATION: Late-twentieth-century author of juvenile and adult fiction, whose novels for teens and preteens are known for their realism.

After publishing *Iggie's House* (1970), her first novel for children, Judy Blume proved a phenomenally popular author of realistic fiction, particularly for children and young adults. The protagonists of her young-adult novels are frequently adolescents who must cope with life-changing experiences while undergoing puberty. Blume's books have been translated into twenty-seven languages and have sold more than seventy million copies worldwide. Her works—often targeted for their occasional use of profanity and frank treatment of puberty and emerging sexuality in teens and preteens—are also among the most frequently challenged in attempts to ban or restrict access to certain books in public and school libraries across the United States.

The Writer's Life

Judy Blume was born Judy Sussman in Elizabeth, New Jersey, on February 12, 1938. She was the second of two children born to Rudolph Sussman, a dentist, and his wife Esther, a homemaker.

Childhood and Adolescent Isolation.

The Sussman household was filled with books. As a child, Blume was allowed to read anything she chose from her mother's personal library.

Blume, who loved to read, was a timid but imaginative child and was always making up stories of her own. In the sixth grade she received an A for a book report she had made up about a book that did not exist.

Blume's older brother was a difficult child, and Blume became determined not to disappoint her parents. She felt pressured to act the part of the perfect child and young woman. In her teens she felt increasingly alone; she told her parents less and less about her true experiences and feelings, always painting a positive picture to please them. Still an avid reader, Blume longed for books that would reflect her own experience and answer her questions about growing up.

College and Marriage.

In college Blume majored in education and planned to be a teacher but felt that she was expected to marry rather than pursue a career. In her sophomore year she met John Blume, a young lawyer. They fell in love and planned to be married. Five weeks before the wedding, Blume's father suffered a fatal heart attack. Jewish tradition required that a wedding date remain fixed even in the event of a death, so Judy and John Blume were married as planned.

Soon after Blume's college graduation, her daughter, Randy, was born, and Blume set aside her plans to teach elementary school. A

Blume, here ten years old in Miami Beach, Florida, used to dream about becoming a cowgirl, a detective, a spy, an actress, and, of course, a ballerina.

second child, Lawrence Andrew (Larry), followed two years later. With no career plans, Blume longed for a creative outlet. After unsuccessful attempts at songwriting and selling cloth banners for children, she decided she would like to write children's stories, beginning with rhyming tales in the style of Dr. Seuss. Blume sent her stories to publishers, but for two years her efforts were rejected.

A Published Writer. Blume enrolled in a New York University class on writing for children and teens. The instructor encouraged Blume and suggested that she try writing long fiction. Blume took the class twice. By the end of the second class she had published two short stories and had written a picture book for young children, *The One in the Middle Is the Green Kangaroo* (1969), which would become her first published book. Thrilled to be accepted as a professional writer, Blume danced across her lawn with the postman who delivered her first check, for twenty dollars.

By this time Blume had also completed a first draft of *Iggie's House* and had responded to a story in the magazine *Writer's Digest* announcing Bradbury Press, a new publishing house seeking authors of realistic children's fiction. Bradbury Press editor Richard Jackson encouraged Blume to rewrite *Iggie's House* and prepare it for publication. As soon as she finished, she began working on *Are You There God? It's Me, Margaret.* (1970), her first book based on her total recall of her own childhood experiences.

This photograph of Blume was taken in the late 1990s by photographer Peter Simon on the island of Martha's Vineyard off the coast of Massachusetts, where Blume has a summerhouse.

HIGHLIGHTS IN BLUME'S LIFE

1938 Judy Blume is born Judy Sussman on February 12 in Elizabeth, New Jersey.

1947 Sussman family spends school year in Miami Beach, Florida; Blume's father remains in New Jersey and commutes.

1956 Blume enrolls in New York University.

1959 Father dies; marries John Blume.

1961 Blume graduates from New York University with a bachelor's degree in education; moves to New Jersey; daughter, Randy, is born.

1963 Son, Lawrence, is born.

1969 Blume publishes first book for children, *The One in the Middle Is the Green Kangaroo*.

1970 Publishes *Iggie's House* and *Are You There God? It's Me, Margaret.*.

1971 Publishes *Then Again, Maybe I Won't* and *Freckle Juice*.

1972 Publishes *Tales of a Fourth-Grade Nothing* and *Otherwise Known as Sheila the Great*, the first two "Fudge" books.

1974 Publishes *Blubber*.

1975 Publishes *Forever . . .*; divorces John Blume.

1976 Marries physicist Thomas Kitchens; moves to New Mexico.

1978 Publishes *Wifey*.

1979 Divorces Kitchens; meets future husband George Cooper.

1981 Publishes *Tiger Eyes*.

1985 Moves to New York City.

1986 Publishes *Letters to Judy: What Your Kids Wish They Could Tell You*.

1987 Marries Cooper; mother dies.

1996 Blume receives American Library Association's Margaret A. Edwards Award.

1998 Publishes *Summer Sisters*.

Published in 1970, *Are You There God? It's Me, Margaret.* became a breakthrough book for Blume. *The New York Times Book Review* listed it among the outstanding children's books of the year, and Blume received countless letters from girls who identified strongly with the novel's young heroine. Although Blume had not set out to cause controversy, some critics believed that her story was marred by the title character's preoccupation with puberty. Between 1970 and 1975 Blume published seven more successful books, including *Then Again, Maybe I Won't* (1971), *Deenie* (1973), and *Blubber* (1974), while critics, parents, and teachers continued to note controversial elements in her stories.

Divorce and Censorship. Blume's success put a strain on her marriage, and she and John Blume were divorced in 1975. A year later Blume married Thomas Kitchens, a physicist, and moved with him to New Mexico. In 1978 Blume published *Wifey*, her first novel written for adults. Critics worried that children would read the sexually explicit *Wifey* simply because it was a Judy Blume book; Blume believed children who attempted it would realize the material was inappropriate for them and set the book aside on their own.

Blume's hasty marriage to Kitchens was unsuccessful, and the couple were divorced in 1979. Soon after her second divorce, Blume met George Cooper, a law professor at Columbia University in New York who later began to write historical crime nonfiction, on a blind date. Cooper and Blume soon began living together and were married in 1987.

During the 1980s Blume's books were frequently challenged by parents who asked that school and public libraries remove her works from their shelves or restrict access so that only older children could read them. Blume published four novels during the 1980s, including *Smart Women* (1983), her second novel for adults. The continuing popularity of her earlier books kept her name high on lists of banned children's authors. When Blume's publisher asked her to remove a few lines about masturbation from *Tiger Eyes* (1981) she complied, but felt that her work had been compromised. In response Blume became deeply involved with the National Coalition Against Censorship (NCAC).

In her nonfiction collection, *Letters to Judy: What Your Kids Wish They Could Tell You* (1986), Blume gathered letters she had received from young fans about problems with parents, stepfamilies, adoption, divorce, peers, siblings, puberty, and abuse. *Letters to Judy* served in a way as a defense of Blume's fiction, proof that real children were familiar with sensitive subjects and eager to discuss them with someone who seemed willing to listen. In *Letters to Judy*, Blume interspersed her young fans' often heartbreaking letters with candid and reassuring stories from her own life, offered friendly advice, and provided a list of organizations and books that might help both parents and children deal with a variety of situations ranging from questions about sexuality to learning disabilities and adoption.

During the 1990s Blume published only two books for children, both sequels to earlier works. *Fudge-a-Mania* (1990) was a third installment of the popular "Fudge" series for young children that she began in 1972, and *Here's to You, Rachel Robinson* (1993) examined more closely the over-achieving title character who first appeared in *Just as Long as We're Together* (1987).

In 1996 Blume was named a distinguished alumna of New York University and honored with the Margaret A. Edwards Award for lifetime achievement from the American Library Association. In 1998 she published *Summer Sisters*, her third adult novel, which drew less on her personal experiences than had her earlier works. In 1999 she edited *Places I Never Meant to Be: Original Stories By Censored Writers*, a collection of short stories written for young people accompanied by authors' comments on censorship. All profits from the book were donated to the NCAC.

The Writer's Work

Judy Blume has produced a broad spectrum of work, including realistic fiction for children, middle-grade readers, and young adults, as well as picture books for young children and novels for adults. She is best known for her novels about preteens and teens, in which adolescents cope with life-changing experiences; her protagonists often describe events and concerns related to puberty or sexuality. Blume generally employs a first-person narrative and writes in simple language that gives her young characters' observations a ring of truth.

Issues in Blume's Fiction. Blume did not intend to write controversial books but merely drew on memories of her own childhood and young adulthood to produce the kind of fiction she wished had been available for her to read when she was growing up. Her work provides information and a point of view that is reassuring to young people who feel alone with their questions about puberty and sexuality. *Are You There God? It's Me, Margaret.* details the concerns Blume remembered from her own days in the sixth grade. Blume wrote *Forever . . .* at her fourteen-year-old daughter's request, to counteract popular fiction for teens that portrayed only negative consequences for young women who were sexually active. *Forever . . .* provides detailed information on how to obtain birth control pills; later editions urge readers to use condoms as protection against sexually transmitted diseases.

Blume's stories often depict a young person dealing with a dramatic change such as divorce, a death in the family, sudden wealth, or simply a move to a new neighborhood. Her characters want to fit in among their peers and sometimes go to great lengths to be part of a group. Friendships are often central to Blume's work, and she frequently writes about successful and unsuccessful communication between friends.

Blume (center) in the early 1990s with some young fans in Paris.

Although characters often believe their friends will make them feel better, they are just as often afraid to confide in them. Blume's fiction also frequently addresses failures of communication and issues of honesty between parents and children.

People in Blume's Fiction. Blume's main characters are usually young people living in middle-class suburbs. Best friends have close, accepting relationships based on shared interests, appreciation of one another's talents, and tolerance of one another's weaknesses; however, Blume's adolescent characters worry about fitting in with their peers and are often afraid to reveal their true thoughts or feelings, even to their closest friends.

Parents are described through their children's eyes and are often fallible. They can be prejudiced, hypocritical, self-absorbed, less than honest, and sometimes unaware of their children's preoccupations and problems. Blume's fictional parents try to do what is right but are not always successful. Grandparents, particularly grandmothers, are often featured characters, offering information, support, or special appreciation of a child that parents may be unable to give.

Important Themes in Blume's Fiction. Blume's most important themes are that all young people must cope with similar problems and that life's difficulties usually cannot be neatly resolved. Her readers learn that their concerns are not unique to them, that puberty and sexuality are normal, that parents make mistakes, that friends can let one another down and still be friends, and that negative experiences are not necessarily disastrous.

Blume avoids neat endings. In her fiction, problems are frequently unresolved and questions are left unanswered. Blume's characters grow up, achieving understanding or acceptance. Children in her books learn that while life and people are not perfect, family relationships and friendships gain strength through surviving a new experience or a crisis.

Controversial Topics. Blume's books have become enormously popular in part because she is willing to deal frankly and nonjudgmentally with sexual issues. For this reason Blume's books have been banned from libraries more often than those of any other children's author. Within the context of her stories, Blume tries to portray honestly what happens during puberty, writing about masturbation, the onset of menstruation, physical development, and interest in sexual activity. Critical discussions of Blume's books for young adults and teens often focus on these issues, although Blume's stories usually center on dramatic changes in her characters' lives rather than sexual issues. The thirteen-year-old hero of *Then Again, Maybe I Won't* experiences the onset of puberty within the context of a story about his family's sudden wealth. *Deenie* is often challenged over the novel's treatment of the subject of masturbation, even though the story centers on how a young woman and her parents cope with her physical condition.

BIBLIOGRAPHY

Blume, Judy, ed. *Places I Never Meant to Be: Original Stories by Censored Writers*. New York: Simon & Schuster, 1999.

_____. "Blume, Judy (Sussman)." In *Something About the Author*. Vol. 79, edited by Kevin S. Hile. New York: Gale Research, 1995.

Garcia-Johnson, R. "Judy Blume." In *Authors and Artists for Young Adults*. Vol. 26, edited by Thomas McMahon. Detroit: Gale Research, 1999.

Gleasner, Diana. "Judy Blume." In *Breakthrough: Women in Writing*. New York: Walker, 1980.

Lee, Betsy. *Judy Blume's Story*. Minneapolis, Minn.: Dillon Press, 1981.

Marcus, Leonard S., and Judy Blume, eds. *Author Talk: Conversations with Judy Blume . . . et al.* New York: Simon & Schuster, 1999.

Maynard, Joyce. "Coming of Age with Judy Blume." *The New York Times Magazine*, December 3, 1978.

Weidt, Maryann N. *Presenting Judy Blume*. Boston: Twayne Publishers, 1990.

Wheeler, Jill C. *Judy Blume*. Edina, Minn.: Abdo & Daughters, 1996.

Wintle, Justin, and Emma Fisher. "Judy Blume." In *The Pied Pipers*. New York: Paddington Press, 1974.

Judy Blume recalls her own childhood experiences vividly in both *Are You There God? It's Me, Margaret.* and *Starring Sally J. Freedman as Herself* (1977). Like Margaret, Blume and her friends formed a club (the "Pre-Teen Kittens") to talk about breasts, boys, and menstruation. Like Margaret's friend Nancy, Blume pretended to get her menstrual period in an effort to fit in with her friends. Margaret's relationship with God is based on Blume's friendly, informal childhood conversations with God.

Starring Sally J. Freedman as Herself is based on a school year Blume spent living in Miami Beach, Florida, with her family just after World War II. Sally's story reflects Blume's close relationship with her own father, her longing for adventure, and her childhood perspective on the war.

Blume's stories for young people are often inspired by her own family or by people she has met or heard about. *Blubber* grew out of an incident that Blume's daughter, Randy, witnessed at school in the fifth grade, in which her classmates locked a girl in a closet and put her on trial. Blume's son was the inspiration for the more lighthearted

The culminating scene where a girl is locked in a school closet in Blume's 1974 novel, *Blubber*, marks a turning point in which the cruelty of classmates is transferred from one victim to another.

"Fudge" books about an outrageous little boy and his exasperated older brother.

Blume wrote *Deenie* after meeting a young girl with scoliosis, a curvature of the spine, and noting that the girl's mother was more upset about the diagnosis than the girl herself. *Deenie* is the only book for which Blume did formal research on the condition and its treatments in addition to drawing on her personal experience and imagination.

Reader's Guide to Major Works

ARE YOU THERE GOD? IT'S ME, MARGARET.

Genre: Novel
Subgenre: Juvenile realistic fiction
Published: New York, 1970
Time period: 1970s; later editions updated
Setting: Suburban New Jersey

Themes and Issues. *Are You There God? It's Me, Margaret.* addresses a sixth-grade girl's concerns as she enters puberty, including menstruation, crushes on boys, first kisses, purchasing a bra, and hoping to develop breasts. Margaret wants to be accepted by her peers. She struggles to conform to her friends' expectations and learns that sometimes they will fail to meet hers. The novel is unusual in its treatment of Margaret's relationship with God and her year-long school project involving her search for a religion. Margaret's prayers are informal and often deal with the same issues she discusses with her young friends. The overlying theme is the preadolescent's desire to fit in and be "normal," as Margaret prays that God will make her just like everyone else.

The Plot. Margaret Simon has moved with her family from New York City to suburban New Jersey. She is befriended by Nancy Wheeler, who invites her to join the Pre-Teen Sensations, a club Nancy has formed with two other friends. The club's rules are that each girl must wear a bra, each must keep a Boy Book listing the boys she likes, and the first girl to menstruate must tell the others everything about it.

Nancy tells Margaret that every family in the neighborhood belongs either to the Jewish Community Center or the Young Men's/Young Women's Christian Association (YM/YWCA). Margaret's mother is a Christian, and her father is Jewish, but neither is practicing. Margaret talks informally to God as a friend,

often praying for her breasts to develop and for help in knowing which religion she should adopt as her own. For a school project, Margaret decides to learn about religions. She visits a synagogue and a church but is bored by the services and tells God that she doesn't feel close to him in either the temple or the church, the way she does when she talks to him herself.

Margaret's friends make fun of their classmate Laura Danker, the first girl in their class

Are You There, God? It's Me, Margaret., Blume's breakthrough novel about a girl's coming-of-age, exploded on the children's book scene in 1970 and was soon after recognized by *The New York Times Book Review* as one of the most outstanding children's books of the year. The book is based on Blume's own childhood experiences.

LONG FICTION

ADULT FICTION

NONFICTION

CHILDREN'S LITERATURE

EDITED TEXT

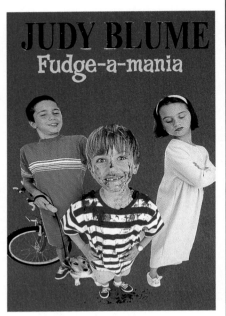

to develop breasts; they tell Margaret that Laura does something unspecified with boys behind the local grocery store. Angry because she has been assigned a dull school project requiring her to work with Laura, Margaret confronts Laura with these rumors and learns that the stories are not true.

Margaret's friend Gretchen is the first of the Pre-Teen Sensations to get her menstrual period. Soon afterward, Nancy tells the other girls that she is also menstruating. While dining out with Nancy's family, Margaret goes to the ladies' room with Nancy and witnesses Nancy's panic at actually getting her first period. Margaret realizes that Nancy lied to her, just as she lied about Laura Danker. Margaret tells God that she will never trust Nancy again.

The story ends when Margaret finally begins menstruating. She is relieved and happy because she will not be the last in her club to menstruate.

Analysis. In Margaret Simon, Judy Blume paints a realistic portrait of an intelligent and thoughtful young girl who wants more than anything to be just like everyone else. Blume's style is simple; Margaret tells her own story in a first-person narrative including often humorous—but never unkind—observations about her friends, classmates, and family. Thirty years after its original publication the book remained extremely popular, although still often challenged because of its subject matter. In typical Blume fashion, Margaret's problems are not all neatly resolved at the end of the book; although she is relieved to be menstruating at last, she has not chosen a religion, and has learned not to believe everything she hears, but to make up her own mind.

SOURCES FOR FURTHER STUDY

Arthur, George W. Review of *Are You There God? It's Me, Margaret.*, by Judy Blume. *Book Window*, Summer 1978.

Russ, Lavinia. Review of *Are You There God? It's Me, Margaret.*, by Judy Blume. *Publishers Weekly*, January 11, 1971.

Siegal, R. A. "Are You There, God? It's Me, Me, Me!: Judy Blume's Self-Absorbed Narrators." *The Lion and the Unicorn*, Fall 1978.

BLUBBER

Genre: Novel
Subgenre: Realistic fiction for preteens
Published: New York, 1974
Time period: 1970s
Setting: Suburban Philadelphia

Themes and Issues. *Blubber* examines the surprising cruelty of children and the ways in which young victims attempt to cope when they become targets of ridicule and abuse. *Blubber* is frequently challenged because the cruelty portrayed goes unpunished. Rather than showing adults intervening or children learning to be sorry for their actions, Blume shows one child allowing herself to be victimized and another successfully standing up for herself.

The Plot. The novel opens with Jill Brenner and her fifth-grade classmates giving reports on mammals. An overweight girl named Linda Fischer reports on whales, focusing on the harvesting and uses of blubber. Wendy, a popular girl, passes a note suggesting that Linda should be called Blubber, and on the school bus home the other children begin taunting Linda with the new nickname.

Inspired by Linda's report, Jill dresses for Halloween as a flenser, a person who peels blubber from whales. Jill, Wendy, and another classmate find Linda in the girls' bathroom at school and threaten to take her clothes off like a flenser stripping blubber from a whale. They lift Linda's skirt and tear at her clothes until she cries, then make her curtsy and kiss Wendy's shoe. Wendy circulates more notes in class encouraging the other children to harass Linda.

The classmates make Linda say "I am Blubber" before they will allow her to drink from the fountain, eat her lunch, or use the toilet. They hold Linda's hands behind her back and lift her skirt to show the boys her underwear, and they force her to eat a piece of chocolate candy after telling her it is really a chocolate-covered ant, causing her to vomit. Jill participates in Linda's torment; she feels that Linda makes herself a target by giving in too easily.

On Halloween night, Jill and her best friend Tracy Wu crush rotten eggs in a neighbor's mailbox. The girls are caught and punished but they are not sorry they egged the mailbox; they feel the neighbor deserved it. Jill decides that Linda must have told on them, and she and Wendy plan to hold a trial and find Linda guilty of tattling.

The idea for *Blubber*, Blume's novel about verbal harassment and physical abuse at the hands of two girls and their followers, came from a story that Blume's daughter told her about a fifth-grade classmate being locked in a closet and put on trial.

The trial is held during the lunch period while the teacher is out of the room. The children lock Linda in a supply closet, but Wendy will not allow Linda a defense lawyer so Jill refuses to participate and releases Linda from the closet. The next day Wendy and the rest of the class have befriended Linda and turned against Jill, now subjecting her to constant ridicule.

Jill tries to laugh with the other children because her mother says that people who can laugh at themselves win respect, but Jill's classmates continue to harass her. Although frightened, Jill stands up to the other girls when they confront her in the girls' bathroom and threaten to undress her. Jill points out that Wendy has not been a loyal friend to the other girls and they desert Wendy, bringing the incident to an end.

Analysis. Although *Blubber* is sometimes challenged because Jill and her fifth-grade classmates use profanity, Blume asserts that early drafts of the book were even more profane. Blume believes that children use such language, and she wants to portray them realistically. In this case she and her editor agreed to cut questionable language that was not important in presenting the true character or story.

Blubber is more often challenged because the cruel children are never caught or punished, and they are not sorry for the things they have done. In the closing chapter Linda has been rejected once again and remains friendless. Jill takes a chance on making a new friend, making a conscious decision that she will not allow her classmates to intimidate or isolate her, nor will she ever go along with such behavior again.

SOURCES FOR FURTHER STUDY

Abramson, Jane. Review of *Blubber*, by Judy Blume. *Library Journal* 99 (November 15, 1974).

Publisher's Weekly. Review of *Blubber*, by Judy Blume. 206, November 25, 1974.

Sutherland, Zena. Review of *Blubber*, by Judy Blume. *Bulletin of the Center for Children's Books*, May, 1975.

FOREVER . . .

 Genre: Novel
 Subgenre: Young-adult fiction
 Published: New York, 1975
 Time period: 1970s
 Setting: Suburban New Jersey

Themes and Issues. Blume's most controversial novel centers on the sexual experiences of a teenage couple who believe that their love will last forever. Blume wrote *Forever . . .* as an alternative to popular young adult fiction portraying the negative consequences of adolescent sexual activity, such as unwanted pregnancy, hasty marriages, and abortion. Katherine, the protagonist of *Forever . . .* , is content with her sexual experience and chooses to end her relationship with her boyfriend because she realizes that she is not ready to make a lasting commitment.

Katherine's parents are portrayed as loving and nonjudgmental; they are concerned about Katherine's single-minded devotion to Michael but do not interfere until the young couple make improbable college plans designed to allow them time together.

The Plot. High school senior Katherine Danziger meets Michael Wagner at a New Year's Eve party. Katherine and Michael are immediately attracted to each other and begin dating. Katherine compares Michael favorably to her former boyfriend Tommy Aronson, who pressured her to have sex; they broke up because she refused. Michael asks Katherine on their second date whether she is a virgin. She asks him to give her time before they become more physically involved, and he agrees.

Michael and Katherine spend a weekend at a ski lodge with Michael's sister and her husband; they sleep together, although Katherine does not want to have intercourse yet. Michael shows Katherine how to stimulate him manually to orgasm, introducing his penis as "Ralph." Michael tells Katherine he loves her, and she responds in kind, promising to love him "forever." They begin meeting at his sister's apartment while she is out of town and soon

This couple sharing a kiss expresses a passion much like Michael and Katherine's in Blume's young-adult novel *Forever . . .* Although Blume makes a strong effort to present a character who carefully considers the pros and cons of a sexual relationship, many consider the novel to be her most controversial.

decide to have sex. At first Katherine insists that Michael use a condom; later she starts using birth control pills.

Katherine's parents express reservations about Katherine's exclusive and intense relationship with Michael, and Katherine's mother warns her that having sex may leave her more vulnerable than she realizes. The young couple make college plans that will allow them to be together frequently but jeopardize Michael's schooling; their parents respond by arranging summer jobs that will force Katherine and Michael to spend several weeks apart. Katherine works as an assistant tennis coach at a summer camp and becomes attracted to the head tennis coach. Michael senses from her letters that something has changed. When he visits Katherine, she admits she has become interested in someone else and has realized that she is not ready to commit herself to someone forever.

Analysis. Blume succeeds in her attempt to show a young woman making a considered decision to become sexually active, approaching it responsibly by using birth control, and suffering no negative repercussions. However, Blume's characterization of Katherine as a strong young woman making her own choices is marred somewhat by repeated scenes in which Michael pressures and playfully manipulates an obviously hesitant Katherine and complains when she refuses him.

Critics have noted the book's instructional qualities, pointing out that *Forever . . .* is as much a how-to manual as it is fiction. Katherine and Michael's sexual activities are explicitly described. Katherine's experience at a Planned Parenthood clinic is described in detail, from her telephone call to make an appointment through the elements of a typical visit: an interview with a social worker, a discussion of birth control, and a standard pelvic exam. For later editions of *Forever . . .*, Blume wrote a brief introduction explaining that using condoms is essential to protect oneself from sexually transmitted diseases such as acquired immunodeficiency syndrome (AIDS) and offering an address and toll-free phone number for Planned Parenthood.

SOURCES FOR FURTHER STUDY

Gough, John. "Reconsidering Judy Blume's Young Adult Novel *Forever . . .*" *The Use of English*, Spring 1985.

Minudri, Regina. Review of *Forever . . .*, by Judy Blume. *School Library Journal* 22 (November 1975).

Rees, David. "Not Even for a One-Night Stand." In *The Marble In the Water*. Boston: The Horn Book, 1980.

Other Works

DEENIE (1973). Thirteen-year-old Deenie's mother expects Deenie to become a model, but her plans are dashed when Deenie is diagnosed with scoliosis, a curvature of the spine. Deenie will have to wear a body brace for the next four years to straighten her spine.

Judy Blume researched scoliosis and its treatment and writes realistically of the frightening and humiliating experience of being fitted for a Milwaukee Brace. The moment-to-moment practical problems of wearing the brace are also examined in detail as Deenie adjusts her wardrobe to accommodate the brace and learns to eat and sleep while wearing it. Deenie is distressed about appearing to be different from her classmates and embarrassed when her first boyfriend touches her, believing that he feels only the fabric and metal of her brace.

Realizing that she needs information and support, Deenie joins a group sponsored by her doctor for people wearing Milwaukee

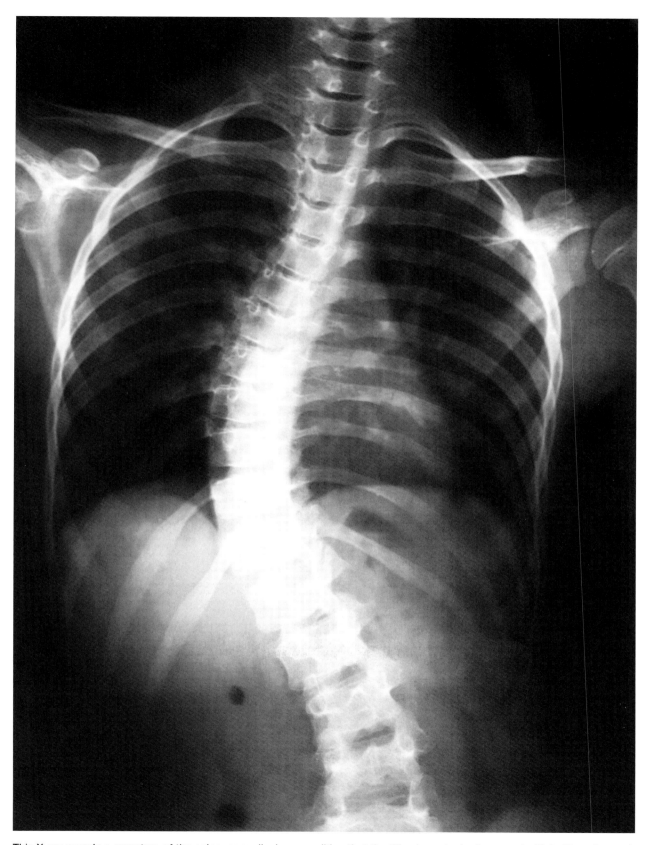

This X-ray reveals a curvature of the spine, or scoliosis, a condition that the title character is diagnosed with in Blume's novel *Deenie*. The idea for *Deenie* emerged after Blume met a fourteen-year-old girl with scoliosis.

Braces. She seeks information about masturbation and sexual intercourse through anonymous question-and-answer sessions offered in physical education classes at her school. *Deenie* has been challenged and banned because of Deenie's interest in sexual matters and because Deenie sometimes copes with stress in her life by masturbating.

IT'S NOT THE END OF THE WORLD

(1972). This novel examines a young girl's efforts to cope with her parents' separation and divorce, focusing on her attempts to understand what is happening to her family and on failures of communication between the child and the adults in her life.

Twelve-year-old Karen Newman knows that her parents are not getting along, but she is stunned when she learns that her father has moved out of the house and her parents are planning to divorce. She cannot understand what has happened between her mother and father, and they are unwilling or unable to try and explain. Karen is left in an information vacuum that she uses her imagination to fill. She first copes by pretending that her parents will not get divorced and that she can find a way to help them reconcile. She does not even confide in her best friend because it is easier to believe that the divorce will not happen if she does not talk about it.

Blume's characters often learn from books or other reading material. Longing for facts and frustrated with her parents' inability to provide concrete information, Karen purchases her own copy of a book about divorce written just for children. The book provides sometimes questionable information, but it is her only resource. Karen realizes that her parents are avoiding each other and tries to get them in a room together so they can see they are making a mistake. When she finally succeeds in bringing her parents together, they have a terrible argument that finally convinces her the divorce is inevitable. She begins to accept this and realizes that she and her family can be happy again.

The solitude of a windswept beach echoes the isolation twelve-year-old Karen Newman experiences when she discovers her parents are planning to divorce in Blume's novel *It's Not the End of the World*.

SUMMER SISTERS

(1998). Blume's most ambitious novel for adults traces the friendship between Vix, a responsible young woman from a troubled family, and the wealthy, adventuresome Caitlin, who first invites Vix to spend the summer with her on the Massachusetts island of Martha's Vineyard when the girls are both twelve. They spend each summer together through high school, experimenting with their sexuality and falling in love with Von and Bru, two young men who work on a construction crew. Caitlin's father and stepmother become surrogate parents and sponsors to Vix, helping her to fulfill her academic potential, attend college, and pursue a career in public relations.

other characters' perspectives, conveys the young girl's fascination with her wild, beautiful, and wealthy friend but fails to show why the adult Vix would tolerate the manipulations of a woman who never grows up—except in Vix's imagination.

THEN AGAIN, MAYBE I WON'T (1971). Thirteen-year-old Tony Miglione lives with his extended family—his father and mother, his grandmother, his older brother Ralph, and Ralph's wife, Angie—in Jersey City, New Jersey. Tony is a normal lower-middle-class boy with a normal life: He has many friends, he likes to play basketball, he runs a paper route, and he looks forward to attending junior high school in the coming fall.

Financial strain on the family moves Tony's father to try and market an electrical device he has invented. Mr. Miglione sells his invention and becomes a partner in an engineering company. Suddenly wealthy, the family moves to a new home in suburban Rosemont, Long Island. Tony's parents worry about what their new neighbors will think of them. They sell their truck because a neighbor asks if workmen are parking a truck in their driveway, and Tony's mother allows another neighbor to call her Carol instead of her given name, Carmella. Tony's brother Ralph gives up the teaching job he loved in order to work for the same company as Mr. Miglione.

Tony befriends his next-door neighbor, Joel Hoober. Tony's mother likes Joel because his family is wealthy and he behaves courteously

This photograph of two girls walking on the beach conveys the warmth of friendship and summertime found in Blume's adult novel *Summer Sisters*, a story that spans almost twenty summers in the lives of two young women.

Caitlin decides to forgo college and instead spends years traveling from place to place, seemingly unable to find a home.

The friendship between the two women is challenged by Caitlin's continual betrayals of Vix and her pursuit of Vix's first boyfriend Bru, whom Caitlin eventually marries. Vix's story, occasionally interrupted by chapters offering in front of her, but Tony sees a different side of the rich, well-mannered young man: Joel habitually shoplifts. Tony is disgusted at the changes in his family, believing that they have given up their values to impress people who have none. He begins to suffer pains in his stomach whenever he is upset.

Tony is eventually hospitalized for his stomach pains and is referred to a psychologist. Tony is unusual for a Blume protagonist in that he is able to freely talk with a psychologist about his feelings. Blume's characters frequently face problems at home or with peers and feel unable to discuss what is happening with anyone, including potentially sympathetic counselors. *Then Again, Maybe I Won't* has often been challenged because of its realistic descriptions of Tony's struggles with the onset of puberty.

After writing *Are You There God? It's Me, Margaret.*, Blume thought it would be interesting to write a book from a thirteen-year-old boy's perspective. She also wondered how a close-knit middle-class family would handle sudden wealth. She quenched both curiosities when she wrote *Then Again, Maybe I Won't*.

Resources

Sources of interest for students of Judy Blume include the following:

Judy Blume's Official Web Site. Maintained by Webmaster George Cooper, Blume's husband, this site offers a biography, photographs, personal interviews, brief descriptions of all Blume's books with her comments on each, Blume's thoughts on writing and censorship, and links to recent articles and interviews available elsewhere on the Web. (http://www.judyblume.com/)

National Coalition Against Censorship. Judy Blume has been very involved with the NCAC, a coalition of over forty organizations working to protect First Amendment rights and fight censorship at the grass-roots level across the United States. The NCAC World Wide Web site includes information about the organization and its programs and articles about current incidents of censorship. (http://www.ncac.org)

Audiotapes. Many of Blume's stories have been recorded and are available in audio form, including *Are You There God? It's Me, Margaret.* (1997), *Freckle Juice* (1986), and four "Fudge" books: *Tales of a Fourth-Grade Nothing* (2000), *Otherwise Known as Sheila the Great* (1997), *Superfudge* (1993), and *Fudge-a-Mania* (2000).

MAUREEN J. PUFFER-ROTHENBERG

Arna Bontemps

BORN: October 13, 1902, Alexandria, Louisiana
DIED: June 4, 1973, Nashville, Tennessee
IDENTIFICATION: A significant figure in twentieth-century African American literature and education for over forty years who was closely associated with the major figures of the Harlem Renaissance.

Bontemps wrote three novels, a collection of stories, a volume of poetry, a play coauthored with Countée Cullen, and numerous works of nonfiction. He wrote nearly twenty books for young readers and edited many collections of black literature. For years he served as head librarian at Fisk University, where he greatly enhanced the black literature holdings, making seminal contributions to the field of African American studies and turning Fisk into a major center for African American research. He assembled the Langston Hughes Collection and gathered valuable papers by Jean Toomer, Countée Cullen, James Weldon Johnson, and Charles S. Johnson for the Fisk Collection. His books for children emphasize the dignity and importance of African American cultural history and helped to preserve it for future generations.

The Writer's Life

Arna Wendell Bontemps, the son of Paul and Marie Pembroke Bontemps, was born on October 13, 1902, in Alexandria, Louisiana. His father, a musician and brickmason, became a lay minister in the Seventh-day Adventist Church after abandoning the Roman Catholic faith in which he had been raised. Bontemps's mother, a teacher, died of pulmonary tuberculosis when he was twelve. In 1906 the family moved to Los Angeles, California, where Bontemps grew up.

The gentle, instructive guidance of a patient teacher is depicted in Henry Ossawa Tanner's 1893 painting, *The Banjo Lesson* (Hampton University Museum, Hampton, Virginia). Bontemps received this type of support from his uncle Buddy, who, unlike his father, encouraged him to write.

Childhood. The Bontemps family settled in the Watts section of Los Angeles, at that time a semirural area. They frequented the farm of Marie's mother, Sara, in Furlough Track, near Watts. When Sara's alcoholic brother Buddy arrived from Louisiana to live with the family in 1910, he and Bontemps became inseparable, somewhat to the father's displeasure. Bontemps's father wanted him to become a fourth-generation brickmason, but his uncle Buddy encouraged him to write instead.

Buddy became a major inspiration to Bontemps. One of the characters in Bontemps's first novel, *God Sends Sunday* (1931), was modeled after Buddy. Frequent visits from Louisiana relatives kept Bontemps connected to his roots. One relative, a railroad porter on the New Orleans–Los Angeles run, visited weekly. During his layovers in Los Angeles, he brought the family current information about Alexandria.

The death of Bontemps's mother in 1914 devastated him. In his later life, he seldom made a speech without referring affectionately and with visible sorrow to his mother. During his grieving process, Bontemps became a voracious reader, escaping into books such as Daniel Defoe's *Robinson Crusoe* (1719), Sir Walter Scott's *Ivanhoe* (1819), and Robert Louis Stevenson's *Treasure Island* (1883) and *Kidnapped* (1886), all of which inspired him greatly. He was a regular at the Watts branch of the Los Angeles Public Library, as well as at the main library, which had a much larger selection. He also read classic authors—William Shakespeare, John Milton, John Donne, and Charles Dickens.

Bontemps (left) with writer and close friend Langston Hughes, date unknown. Bontemps and Hughes worked on several projects together.

Education and Teaching Career. Three years after Bontemps's mother's death, his father enrolled him in the private, mostly white San Fernando Academy. He warned his son not to flaunt his "Negro-ness" at this school. Upon graduating from the San Fernando Academy in 1920, Bontemps entered Pacific Union College, an Adventist institution from which he received his bachelor's degree in 1923.

He then moved to New York City, embarking on a teaching career at New York City's Harlem Academy, where he taught from 1924 until 1931, the year in which his first novel, *God Sends Sunday*, was published. Bontemps figured importantly in the Harlem Renaissance, a major literary and cultural movement that attracted America's most prominent black writers.

In 1931 Bontemps and his schoolteacher wife, Alberta Johnson, whom he had married in 1926, moved to Huntsville, Alabama, where he taught English at Oakwood Junior College until 1934. During this period, he began writing children's books. Determined to present black cul-

ture to young readers, he felt he could make his greatest social impact by informing black children of their cultural heritage.

From 1934 until 1937, the year after the publication of his second novel, *Black Thunder* (1936), Bontemps taught at Chicago's Shiloh Academy. He left Shiloh to work in the Illinois Writers Project, part of the New Deal's Works Progress Administration. During his stint there, he met Jack Conroy, who became his frequent collaborator.

After receiving a Rosenwald Fellowship in 1938, Bontemps traveled in the Caribbean, the scene of his next novel, *Drums at Dusk* (1939). He was granted another Rosenwald Fellowship in 1942 and was able to pursue a master's degree in library science at the University of Chicago while continuing his research on black writers in Illinois. He received his master's degree in 1943 and became full professor and head librarian at Fisk University in Nashville, Tennessee, where he spent most of his remaining years.

HIGHLIGHTS IN BONTEMPS'S LIFE

1902	Arna Wendell Bontemps is born on October 13 in Alexandria, Louisiana.
1906	Family moves to Los Angeles, California.
1917–1920	Bontemps attends San Fernando Academy.
1923	Receives bachelor's degree from Pacific Union College.
1924	Begins teaching at Harlem Academy in New York City; first poem, "Hope," is published.
1926	Marries Alberta Johnson; wins Pushkin Prize for "Golgotha Is a Mountain."
1927	Wins Pushkin Prize for "The Return."
1931	First novel, *God Sends Sunday*, is published; begins teaching at Oakwood Junior College in Huntsville, Alabama.
1932	Receives *Opportunity* short story prize for "A Summer Tragedy."
1934	Begins teaching at Chicago's Shiloh Academy.
1936	Publishes *Black Thunder*.
1938	Receives Rosenwald Fellowship; travels in Caribbean.
1942	Receives Rosenwald Fellowship to pursue "Negro in Illinois" project; attends University of Chicago.
1943	Granted master of library science degree by the University of Chicago; appointed full professor and head librarian at Fisk University.
1946	*St. Louis Woman*, dramatic collaboration with Countée Cullen, is produced.
1947	Bontemps is awarded Guggenheim Fellowship.
1954	Granted second Guggenheim Fellowship.
1956	Wins Jane Addams Children's Book Award for *The Story of the Negro* (1948).
1966	Begins teaching literature and history at University of Illinois, Chicago.
1967	Shares James L. Dow Award for *Anyplace but Here* (1966) with collaborator Jack Conroy.
1969	Awarded honorary Doctor of Humane Letters degree by Morgan State University; is appointed writer-in-residence at Fisk University.
1972	Appointed honorary Library of Congress consultant in American cultural history.
1973	Receives honorary doctorate from Berea College; dies on June 4 in Nashville, Tennessee.

The Later Years. From 1943 until his death in 1973, Bontemps lived mostly in Nashville, but he spent the years from 1966 to 1969 teaching at the University of Illinois in Chicago and the 1971 academic year at Yale University in Connecticut as visiting professor of Afro-American studies and curator of the James Weldon Johnson Collection. He always returned, however, to Fisk, where he built a fine collection of black literature and established the Langston Hughes Collection. He felt comfortable at Fisk and counted its president, Charles Spurgeon Johnson, among his closest friends.

Bontemps's efforts turned Fisk University into a major center for African American research. Although in his early years Bontemps showed limited interest in African American culture, he eventually created an indispensable resource for literary scholars. He also helped to preserve a record of African American culture for future generations in the children's books he wrote himself.

The Final Years. Two events in 1967 forced Bontemps to face his own mortality. Within one week, death came to Langston Hughes, Bontemps's close friend for over thirty years, and to John Wesley Work III, a fraternity brother and colleague at Fisk, among his closest friends in Nashville. Bontemps and his wife flew from Chicago to Nashville for Work's funeral, then rushed to the airport for a flight to New York City to attend Hughes's funeral the following day.

Although Bontemps worked steadily for the next six years, the memory of his friends' deaths clouded his days. During these six years, he received awards for his writing. Two honorary doctorates were bestowed upon him. Fisk appointed him writer-in-residence in 1969; he became an honorary consultant to the Library of Congress in 1972. Shortly after being awarded an honorary doctorate by Berea College in Kentucky, Bontemps had a heart attack and died suddenly in Nashville on June 4, 1973. His wife and six adult children survived him.

SOME INSPIRATIONS BEHIND BONTEMPS'S WORK

Early personal influences played a major part in shaping Arna Bontemps's work. Chief among these were his mother, whose death in 1914 severely upset him; his maternal grandmother, Sara Ward Pembroke, who lived to be over one hundred years old; and his uncle Buddy, who, unlike his father, encouraged his writing.

After 1924, the writers of the Harlem Renaissance inspired Bontemps significantly, particularly Langston Hughes, Countée Cullen, and Jack Conroy, with each of whom he collaborated. Alain Locke, a leader and chief interpreter of the Harlem Renaissance, was another inspiration to him, as was sociologist Charles Spurgeon Johnson, president of Fisk University during Bontemps's tenure there.

Bontemps drew inspiration from his reading of authors such as William Shakespeare, Sir Walter Scott, Daniel Defoe, Robert Louis Stevenson, and especially Alexandre Dumas, also known as *père,* a seventeenth-century French novelist and playwright. During his residence in New York, he was inspired by Walt Whitman's *Leaves of Grass* (various editions published 1855 to 1892), as was his frequent collaborator, Langston Hughes. Bontemps's and Hughes's collaboration "I, Too, Sing America" reflects this influence.

The Writer's Work

Arna Bontemps knew literature. He had a habit of reading everything he could lay his hands on, and he also completed the residency and foreign language requirements for a doctorate in English at the University of Chicago, although he never completed the required dissertation.

Finding an Audience. Bontemps published three novels between 1931 and 1939 but was convinced that he could make his greatest contribution to black culture and to African American society by writing books for young people who had not yet developed the disillusionment that characterized many blacks in his own generation. His first children's book,

Popo and Fifina: Children of Haiti (1932), a collaboration with Langston Hughes, recounts the daily lives of two black children in Haiti as their father leaves farming, moves to the coast, and begins a new life as a fisherman. This book is extraordinarily well written; its prose passages verge at times on poetry. It was well received and filled a wide gap in children's literature in the United States, which generally focused on white children in middle-class settings. The success of *Popo and Fifina* encouraged Bontemps greatly and spurred him to write two more children's books, *You Can't Pet a Possom* (1934) and *Sad-Faced Boy* (1937).

Over the next thirty-five years, Bontemps

Jean Chery's painting *Pastoral Family* illustrates life on a farm in Haiti, the setting of Bontemps's first children's book, *Popo and Fifina: Children of Haiti*. Haiti is also the setting of Bontemps's second historical novel, *Drums at Dusk*.

EDITED TEXTS

1941   Golden Slippers: An Anthology of Negro Poetry for Young Readers
1949   The Poetry of the Negro, 1746–1949 (with Hughes)
1958   The Book of Negro Folklore (with Hughes)
1960   The Autobiography of an Ex-Colored Man (by James Weldon Johnson; edited and with an introduction by Bontemps)
1963   American Negro Poetry
1969   Great Slave Narratives
1969   Hold Fast to Dreams: Poems Old and New
1971   The Poetry of the Negro, 1746–1970
1972   The Harlem Renaissance Remembered

NONFICTION

1941   Father of the Blues (with W. C. Handy)
1945   They Seek a City (with Jack Conroy)
1961   One Hundred Years of Negro Freedom
1966   Anyplace but Here (with Conroy)
1971   Free at Last: The Life of Frederick Douglass
1980   Arna Bontemps-Langston Hughes Letters, 1925–1967, ed. Charles H. Nichols

CHILDREN'S LITERATURE

1932   Popo and Fifina: Children of Haiti (with Langston Hughes)
1934   You Can't Pet a Possum
1937   Sad-Faced Boy
1942   The Fast Sooner Hound (with Conroy)
1945   We Have Tomorrow
1946   Slappy Hooper: The Wonderful Sign Painter (with Conroy)
1948   The Story of the Negro
1951   Sam Patch: The High, Wide, and Handsome Jumper (with Conroy)
1951   Chariot in the Sky: A Story of the Jubilee Singers
1954   The Story of George Washington Carver
1955   Lonesome Boy
1959   Frederick Douglass: Slave, Fighter, Freeman
1964   Famous Negro Athletes
1970   Mr. Kelso's Lion
1972   Young Booker: Booker T. Washington's Early Days
1997   The Pasteboard Bandit

LONG FICTION

1931   God Sends Sunday
1936   Black Thunder
1939   Drums at Dusk

SHORT FICTION

1973   The Old South: "A Summer Tragedy" and Other Stories of the Thirties

POETRY

1963   Personals

PLAYS

1946   St. Louis Woman (with Countée Cullen)
1949   Free and Easy (adaptation of St. Louis Woman)

Popo and Fifina
CHILDREN OF HAITI
Arna Bontemps & Langston Hughes

Introduction & Afterword by Arnold Rampersad

wrote more than a dozen books for children and adolescents. These ranged from biographies, such as *The Story of George Washington Carver* (1954), *Frederick Douglass: Slave, Fighter, Freeman* (1959), *Free at Last: The Life of Frederick Douglass* (1971), and *Young Booker: Booker T. Washington's Early Days* (1972), to a collection of stories about the careers of successful blacks, *We Have Tomorrow* (1945). Some reviewers criticized Bontemps for neglecting to write about the intellectual lives of his subjects, but he did not feel that such an emphasis was entirely appropriate for his intended young adult audience.

Use of Language. Bontemps was exposed to the black dialect and to the Creole dialect of Louisiana, where he and his relatives had lived. The authenticity of his language was universally praised. His earliest prize-winning poems, "Golgotha Is a Mountain," "The Return," and "Nocturne at Bethesda," captured with convincing realism the cadences and vocabulary of black people.

This authenticity of language carried over into his novels, particularly *Black Thunder*, his most successful work of long fiction. His accurate use of language distinguishes the fourteen stories in his collection *The Old South* (1973), which contains his most frequently anthologized story, "A Summer Tragedy" (1932).

Based on his novel *God Sends Sunday*, the play *St. Louis Woman*, a collaboration with Countée Cullen, ran on Broadway for 113 performances in 1946. Critics generally commended Bontemps for capturing the language of black people convincingly. In 1949 the play had a successful run in Amsterdam under the title *Free and Easy*; its reviewers seldom failed to mention the realism of its language.

Thematic Emphases. Throughout his writing, Bontemps demonstrated the dignity and humanity of African Americans. In order to inspire young people, he wrote biographies of such outstanding black leaders as George Washington Carver, Booker T. Washington, and Frederick Douglass. He also wrote about some of the more difficult issues in black life and history. Gabriel Prosser, the revolutionary protagonist of *Black Thunder*, was a heroic slave who resisted his oppressors, staged a rebellion, and was killed for his valiant actions. Bontemps's celebrated short story "A Summer Tragedy" focuses on the plight of a black sharecropper and his wife who, having lost their five children and suffering from the infirmities of age, consider suicide the only solution to their problems.

Bontemps focuses not only on blacks in the United States but also on blacks in Haiti, as in *Popo and Fifina* and *Drums at Dusk*, a novel about an eighteenth-century Haitian slave uprising. This book and *Black Thunder* anticipated the themes of William Styron's *The Confessions of Nat Turner* (1967), published over thirty years later.

BIBLIOGRAPHY

Baker, Houston A., Jr. *Black American Literature in America*. New York: McGraw-Hill, 1971.

Barksdale, Richard, and Keneth Kinnamon, eds. *Black Writers in America*. New York: Macmillan, 1972.

Bone, Robert. *The Negro Novel in America*. New Haven, Conn.: Yale University Press, 1965.

Brown, Sterling. *The Negro in American Fiction*. Washington, D.C.: Associates in Negro Folk Education, 1937.

Fleming, Robert E. *James Weldon Johnson and Arna Wendell Bontemps: A Reference Guide*. Boston: G. K. Hall, 1978.

Jones, Kirkland C. *Renaissance Man from Louisiana: A Biography of Arna Wendell Bontemps*. Westport, Conn.: Greenwood Press, 1992.

Nichols, Charles H., ed. *Arna Bontemps-Langston Hughes Letters, 1925–1967*. New York: Dodd, Mead, 1980.

Singh, Amritjit. *The Novels of the Harlem Renaissance: Twelve Black Writers, 1923–1933*. University Park: Pennsylvania State University Press, 1976.

Sundquist, Eric J. *The Hammers of Creation: Folk Culture in Modern African-American Fiction*. Athens: University of Georgia Press, 1992.

Whitlow, Roger. *Black American Literature: A Critical History*. Totowa, N.J.: Littlefield, Adams, 1974.

Reader's Guide to Major Works

BLACK THUNDER

Genre: Novel
Subgenre: Historical chronicle
Published: New York, 1936
Time period: 1800
Setting: Richmond, Virginia

Themes and Issues. Arna Bontemps chose to write about one of the most pressing social and political issues in the nineteenth-century United States—slavery and its consequences. He is concerned with such problems as the complacency or defeatism of some slaves, the yearning for freedom among others, and the dangers inherent in trying to buck a system firmly in place and legally sanctioned throughout the southern states at the time in which the novel is set, 1800.

To sustain these themes, Bontemps selected a group of characters, black and white, that represents a cross-section of the current society. His microcosm includes black farmers, laborers, house servants, and free blacks as well as white slave owners and some whites who oppose slavery but have to tread lightly in showing their opposition to it. The atmosphere that grows out of this microcosm is, understandably, one of distrust and suspicion.

Winslow Homer's 1876 painting *A Visit from the Old Mistress* mirrors Bontemps's restraint to cast judgment on his characters. While Homer leaves much to the viewer's discretion, Bontemps permits only the actions of his characters to mold the reader's opinion.

The Plot. Bontemps wove his story around an actual slave rebellion that took place in Virginia in 1800 after the whipping to death of a black slave, Bundy, by his tyrannical owner. Gabriel Prosser, a slave, draws other slaves into his plot to gain freedom by overpowering and overthrowing the slaveholders. A free black, Mingo, finds biblical justifications for such an insurrection. Other blacks who join Prosser look for portents in nature to predict success and seek means of conjuring impediments to evil spirits who might thwart their rebellion.

Prosser masses over one thousand people, mostly slaves, to support him and his forces on the night of the scheduled rebellion. The plan is for three columns of slaves to lay siege to the arsenal in Richmond, arm themselves with guns and ammunition, and then gather at a staging area. A cadre of trusted supporters is then to fan out to nearby towns in Henrico and other nearby counties, spreading the word and recruiting slaves to join the rebellion.

The attack, however, is thwarted when a heavy rainstorm engulfs the area, making it difficult for Prosser's forces to advance through the woods. Some of the slaves consider the storm a premonition of doom. The weather is so daunting that the original band of over one thousand shrinks significantly by the time Prosser reaches Richmond. He has no alternative but to cancel the attack.

Melody, a mulatto woman who has conferred sexual favors on black and white men alike, uses her influence to get Prosser to board a ship to Norfolk. When he arrives there, however, he does not have the spirit to run any further. He turns himself in, is returned to Richmond, and is eventually hanged, as are many other slaves connected with the uprising.

Analysis. *Black Thunder*'s protagonist is a thirty-year-old slave, Gabriel Prosser, treated by his master much like any other property—a horse, a piece of furniture, or an acre of land. A slave like Prosser is permitted little personal life. He can be sold at his owner's slightest whim and, if he has a family, can be wrested away and forever separated from it. Bontemps does not portray the white slaveholders, such as Moseley Sheppard, as villains, but rather as people who merely live according to social convention, accepting unquestioningly their God-given right as affluent whites to own and totally control other humans.

Ben and Pharaoh, both slaves who support Prosser in his rebellion, buckle under the pressure imposed by white society when news of the rebellion leaks out. They become betrayers, although it is difficult to judge them harshly, because of the terrifying personal consequences of their silence. Mingo, a free black who lives in Richmond, is in a less tenable position than most of the other blacks in the novel. He sympathizes with Prosser and his cause but has much to lose if he sides too openly with the dissidents. Having won his freedom, he is understandably unwilling to jeopardize it.

In this story, as in all of his work, Bontemps is a master of restraint; he avoids making value judgments about his characters' actions. He portrays his black characters as multidimensional, although his white characters are somewhat more stereotypically rendered. The characters, through their actions, speak for themselves implicitly and explicitly. Gabriel Prosser is particularly well drawn without being glorified. He is not an exceptional man, but his utter dedication to the cause of freedom leads and inspires others.

SOURCES FOR FURTHER STUDY

Bader, Barbara. "History Changes Color: A Story in Three Parts." *Horn Book Magazine* 73 (January/February 1997).

Barksdale, Richard, and Keneth Kinnamon, eds. *Black Writers in America*. New York: Macmillan, 1972.

Jones, Kirkland C. *Renaissance Man from Louisiana: A Biography of Arna Wendell Bontemps*. Westport, Conn.: Greenwood Press, 1992.

Weil, Dorothy. "Folklore Motifs in Arna Bontemps's *Black Thunder*." *Southern Folklore Quarterly* 35 (March 1971).

DRUMS AT DUSK

Genre: Novel
Subgenre: Historical chronicle
Published: New York, 1939
Time period: Late eighteenth century
Setting: Haiti

Themes and Issues. As in Bontemps's first historical novel, *Black Thunder*, this second historical novel portrays black slaves' passionate desire for freedom. In a 1936 speech Bontemps told of how, in his earliest school days in California, he wondered why black slaves had not risen up to demand their freedom. As he matured, he explored this question, becoming fascinated with recorded slave insurrections, including the one led by Gabriel Prosser, which Bontemps described in *Black Thunder*.

Both *Black Thunder* and *Drums at Dusk* present slaves whose overwhelming wish is to be free. The escape-and-revolt theme is evident early in *Drums at Dusk*. Bontemps also describes slave characters who have been co-opted body and soul by the institution of slavery. They have been raised in bondage and do not know any other way of life. They accept their oppression stoically and dream of a better life in the afterworld, in which most of them staunchly believe.

The Plot. In late eighteenth-century Haiti, Bontemps notes that the black slave population outnumbered the white plantation owners by almost ten to one. The only way in which whites could maintain their control was through intimidation and by pitting the slaves against the mulattos, of whom there were many, due to the sexual dalliances of white masters, many of whom preferred their black or light-skinned mistresses to their socially accepted white wives. It was common for some white slaveholders to flaunt their dark mistresses openly. The children born of these unions were often given favored positions as house servants.

As social tensions escalated because of the internal struggles among the wealthy plantation owners, the lower-class whites who did not own slaves, and the favored mulattos,

Haitian slaves became restive. In 1796 Toussaint-Louverture became governor-general of St. Domingue (later named Haiti). In 1801, the time in which the novel is set, Toussaint-Louverture's forces defeated the Spanish forces that controlled the area. All of the slaves were freed, and Toussaint-Louverture gained control of the entire island of Hispaniola.

Toussaint-Louverture, sympathetic to the black insurrection that took place in Haiti, helped wrest power from the whites, who had oppressed the black population and gained political control of Haiti. A French invasion began in 1802. Toussaint-Louverture surrendered to

Bontemps's historical novel *Drums at Dusk* is based on General Toussaint-Louverture's real-life struggle to emancipate Haiti. This silk screen-on-paper panel by artist Jacob Lawrence features Toussaint-Louverture and is one of forty-one panels in Lawrence's *Toussaint L'Ouverture* series.

The anguish etched on the face of a tenant farmer in Elizabeth Catlett's 1970 linocut *Sharecropper* resembles the distress experienced by an older sharecropper and his wife in Bontemps's short story "A Summer Tragedy."

the French in May on the condition that slavery would not be restored. *Drums at Dusk* recounts the struggle for freedom that, in the end, cost Toussaint-Louverture, imprisoned in a French dungeon, his life.

Analysis. Although *Drums at Dusk* was not received as enthusiastically as *Black Thunder*, it is important because it explores and promotes the theme of self-determination among human beings of all classes and colors. Macmillan, the book's publisher, thought well enough of it to issue a British edition in 1940.

In *Drums at Dusk*, as in *Black Thunder*, Bontemps raises the notion that blacks had advocates outside the institution of slavery as early as the late 1700s. Abolitionists from both New England and Europe stood ready to help them gain their freedom. Their early and various uprisings, though bloody and at times seemingly futile, paved the way for their eventual emancipation.

SOURCES FOR FURTHER STUDY

Cooke, Michael G. *Afro-American Literature in the Twentieth Century: The Achievement of Intimacy.* New Haven, Conn.: Yale University Press, 1984.

Davis, Arthur P. *From the Dark Tower: Afro-American Writers, 1900–1960.* Washington, D.C.: Howard University Press, 1974.

Gloster, Hugh M. *Negro Voices in American Fiction.* Chapel Hill: North Carolina University Press, 1948.

Other Works

FREE AT LAST: THE LIFE OF FREDERICK DOUGLASS (1971). In his attempt to introduce successful black role models to young people, Arna Bontemps produced a highly readable biography of Frederick Douglass. This book is an outgrowth of his earlier children's book, *Frederick Douglass: Slave, Fighter, Freeman.* Bontemps felt such a kinship to Douglass that he wrote with considerable facility about the latter's life, sometimes inventing situations to meet his artistic needs. Many who have read this book directed specifically to adolescents have considered it a historically based novel rather than a biography.

Bontemps does not write analytically about Douglass's intellectual development; rather, he captures much of the excitement and magic of Douglass's intriguing existence, emphasizing the obstacles Douglass had to overcome as a black man and showing what practical means he employed to overcome them.

This biography is engaging from cover to cover; it is an obvious labor of love and a measure of Bontemps's racial commitment. Bontemps realized the necessity for young black people to learn about blacks in American history who overcame racial prejudice to make worthwhile contributions to society in general, not merely to black society.

GOD SENDS SUNDAY (1931). Bontemps's first novel, *God Sends Sunday,* focuses on Little Augie, a famous jockey vaguely reminiscent of Bontemps's Uncle Buddy, and his exploits. In its Mississippi River Valley setting, the book departs from much of the writing of the Harlem Renaissance, which is usually set in New York City.

The plot emphasizes sex and the fast living of the Roaring Twenties. It is often compared to Carl Van Vechten's *Nigger Heaven* (1926). The women in Bontemps's novel are presented largely as sex objects; most of them can be had for a price. The men settle most of their differences with knives. The book was attacked by such prominent black figures as W. E. B. Du Bois, who objected to its presentation of black society but admitted that the protagonist was skillfully portrayed.

"GOLGOTHA IS A MOUNTAIN" (1926). This poem, which brought Bontemps the Alexander Pushkin Poetry Prize of *Opportunity* magazine in 1926, is typical of poetry of the Harlem Renaissance. In it, Bontemps expresses the longing of blacks for their African roots. Langston Hughes expressed similar sentiments in his celebrated poem "The Negro Speaks of Rivers" (1925). "Golgotha Is a Mountain" expresses the remarkable capacity of African Americans for survival and describes their determined endurance, even when the odds are against them, as they were in the United States for many years.

"A SUMMER TRAGEDY" (1932). In this sensitive and verbally economic short story, Bontemps tells the story of an elderly black sharecropper, Jeff Patton, and his frail, blind wife, Jennie. Jeff has had a stroke and fears that another one might leave him helpless with only Jennie to look after him. The couple lose all five of their children over a two-year period. The children's deaths are not described, in order to keep the required focus centered on Jeff and Jennie.

The pair dress up in their best clothes, get into Jeff's Model-T Ford, and set out toward the river. It is clear that they are quickly reaching the end of their resources. After a few delays and some question about whether they should carry out the mission on which both have decided, Jeff accelerates, driving his automobile over a cliff and into the raging river, where both he and Jennie die.

Resources

An extensive selection of Arna Bontemps's papers and a treasure trove of papers relating to him is found in the George Arents Research Library of Syracuse University. Bontemps's correspondence with Langston Hughes, published in Charles Nichols's *Arna Bontemps-Langston Hughes Letters, 1925-1967*, is held in Yale University's James Weldon Johnson Collection, of which Bontemps was curator in 1971. The Special Collections Department of the Fisk University Library holds many of Bontemps's papers, including tapes relating the oral history and folklore of blacks, interviews, letters, photographs, and manuscripts, many of which are edited in Bontemps's hand.

Arna Bontemps African American Museum and Cultural Arts Center. Bontemps's boyhood home in Alexandria, Louisiana, was made into a museum in 1988, and it features tours, exhibits, and cultural events. The museum's Web site has links to other museums and organizations devoted to African American culture. (http://www.arnabontempsmuseum.com/Default.htm)

Arna Wendell Bontemps (1902–1973): Teacher Resource File. This page at the Internet School Library Media Center Web site features a Bontemps biography, a bibliography, texts of his work, and lesson plans. The museum's Web site links to other related museums and organizations. (http://falcon.jmu.edu/~ramseyil/bontemps.htm)

Smithsonian Folkways Recordings. Arna Bontemps read a number of poems that were recorded by Folkways Records in the 1950s. Some have been reissued by Smithsonian Folkways, including *An Anthology of African American Poetry for Young People* (1990). Other Smithsonian Folkways reissues of Bontemps recordings include *An Anthology of Negro Poets in the U.S.A.: 200 Poems* (1988) and *Smithsonian Folkways Children's Music Collection* (1998).

R. BAIRD SHUMAN

Gwendolyn Brooks

BORN: June 7, 1917, Topeka, Kansas
DIED: December 3, 2000, Chicago, Illinois
IDENTIFICATION: Late-twentieth-century poet best known for mastery of technique and form in her presentation of daily life as a means to reveal black identity and the problems of social injustice and hypocrisy.

A prolific poet and occasional prose writer, Gwendolyn Brooks published her first collections of poetry shortly after the end of World War II. Her works captured the variety of personalities in the African American community and family, giving special attention to the coming-of-age of a young black woman. Later works explored instances of racial injustice and celebrated African American heroes. In 1950 Brooks was the first African American to win the Pulitzer Prize, for *Annie Allen* (1949). In 1968 she was named Poet Laureate of Illinois, after the death of Carl Sandburg. From 1985 to 1986 Brooks served as poetry consultant to the Library of Congress. She is the recipient of numerous other awards and honors and is nationally recognized as a poet of lively humor, subtle satire, and sobering good sense.

The Writer's Life

Gwendolyn Brooks was born in Topeka, Kansas, on June 7, 1917. She was the daughter of David Anderson Brooks and Keziah Wims Brooks, who both traced their ancestry to blacks who migrated north to Kansas after the end of the Civil War. Brooks's father was born in Acheson, Kansas, the son of a runaway slave named Lucas Brooks. David Brooks was the only child of twelve siblings to complete high school. He aspired to be a physician and attended Fisk University, but economic hardships necessitated his full-time employment as a janitor. Brooks's mother, Keziah Wims, studied at Emporia State Normal School and subsequently taught elementary school classes. The family took up residence in the Hyde Park area of Chicago, Illinois.

Childhood. After the birth of Brooks's brother, Raymond, the family moved to a larger apartment at Fifty-sixth Street and Lake Park Avenue, where the children had space to play in a garden. David Brooks assumed the role of breadwinner, while Keziah dedicated herself to raising the children and cultivating a garden. Both parents encouraged Brooks to pursue her interest in language: Her father provided her with a practical writing desk, and her mother declared that Gwendolyn might become "the lady Paul Laurence Dunbar." Brooks studied literature in school, developing a familiarity with the British Romantic poets; the Chicago writers, such as Carl Sandburg and Edgar Lee Masters; and the Harlem Renaissance writers, such as Paul Laurence Dunbar, Langston Hughes, and Countée Cullen.

The Emerging Artist. During her high school years, Brooks met the prominent black writers James Weldon Johnson and Langston Hughes. Spurred by Johnson's suggestion that she study modern writers, Brooks read the work of T. S. Eliot, Ezra Pound, and E. E. Cummings. Brooks met Langston Hughes at the Metropolitan Community Church. Hughes read the pack of poems that Brooks had with her and urged her to think seriously of a writing career.

Brooks on the back steps of her home in Chicago, Illinois, in 1960. Although Brooks accepted many teaching assignments in other cities, she was never away from her much-loved hometown of Chicago for long.

Brooks achieved early success in her writing, publishing her first poem, "Eventide," in *American Childhood* in 1930. After graduating from Englewood High school in 1934, she worked on the staff of the *Chicago Defender*, in which she published several poems in a weekly poetry column called "Lights and Shadows." She completed a course of study at Wilson Junior College in 1936.

At a meeting of the Youth Council of the National Association for the Advancement of Colored People (NAACP) she met Henry Lowington Blakely II, with whom she shared an interest in writing. The couple were married on September 17, 1939, and moved into a small kitchenette apartment. This living experience later proved to be the inspiration for Brooks's first collection of poems, *A Street in Bronzeville* (1945). The couple had a son, Henry Blakely, Jr., in 1940.

In 1941 Brooks and Blakely attended a poetry workshop with Inez Cunningham Stark, who insisted on diligent study of the modern writers and advocated a taste for subtlety and originality in method and idea. Through guided revision at the workshop, Brooks developed some of the poems that later appeared in *A Street in Bronzeville*. She submitted poems to an editor at Alfred A. Knopf, Emily A. Morison, who called for further revision. Brooks also submitted her work to Harper & Row, where it was eventually reviewed by the prominent African American author Richard Wright, who suggested that an additional long poem be added to the collection. Brooks completed "The Sundays of Satin Legs Smith," and the completed manuscript was published as *A Street in Bronzeville* in 1945.

Achieving a National Reputation. From 1946 to 1947 Brooks continued her writing with the support of two consecutive Guggenheim Fellowships. She began to focus on the life of a particular young female, tracing the maturation of a character named Annie Allen from childhood into adolescence and from womanhood into motherhood. *Annie*

Giuseppe Ar's 1929 painting *The Desk* represents Brooks's love and admiration for her father, who encouraged her to write by providing her with a practical writing desk at an early age. In a poem she wrote for her father, she supplied her own epitaph: *He who was Goodness, Gentleness, / And Dignity is free, / Translates to public Love / Old private charity.*

Allen was published in 1949, and, in 1950, the book won a Pulitzer Prize in Poetry, making Brooks the first African American writer to win a Pulitzer Prize. In 1951 Brooks's second child, Nora, was born.

Brooks's career flourished, and she continued to publish for Harper & Row. In 1953 she published a fictional autobiography, *Maud Martha*. In 1956 she completed *Bronzeville Boys and Girls*, a collection aimed at a juvenile audience. Greatly moved by the death of her father, the death of Inez Cunningham Stark, and the struggle for civil rights in the South, Brooks completed *The Bean Eaters* in 1960. With ever-strengthening control of style and tone, she captured both the dignity and the quiet desperation of anonymous blacks as well as the horrifying events connected with Little Rock and Emmett Till, a fourteen-year-old black boy who was murdered in Mississippi in 1955.

The Turning Point. Brooks's successes mounted as she accepted teaching positions at Columbia College in Chicago, the City University of New York, Columbia University in New York, and the University of Wisconsin-Madison. Her previous works were gathered in collections, such as *Selected Poems* (1963) and *The World of Gwendolyn Brooks* (1971).

In April 1967, Brooks attended a conference for African American writers at Fisk University and recognized a powerful transformation taking place in her life and art. Writers such as Amiri Baraka and Haki R. Madhubuti helped Brooks address the question of black writers writing about black people for a black readership. Soon Brooks found it necessary to drop her connection with Harper & Row and pursue publication with smaller independent presses operated by writers such as Dudley Randall, Madhubuti, and Brooks herself. Her works *In the Mecca* (1968) and *Report from Part One: An Autobiography* (1972) were written in this new spirit and published through these new channels.

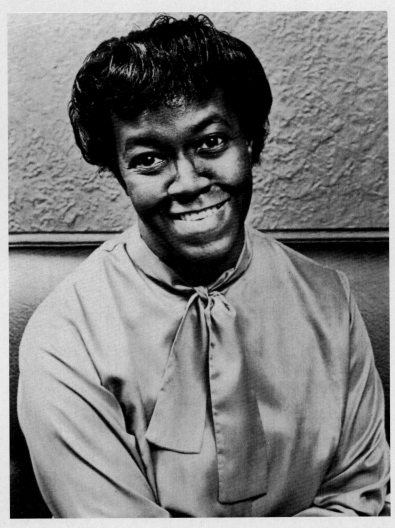

This photograph of Brooks was taken in the 1960s, a decade that marked a major turning point in her career. She decided to discontinue her relationship with the mainstream publishing house Harper & Row, opting to be published by smaller presses that focused more on black consciousness.

The Ongoing Commitment. Throughout the latter half of the twentieth century, Brooks remained dedicated to black consciousness and independent publishing. Although her abandonment of mainstream publication was risky, she proved triumphant, traveling throughout the country, giving readings and lectures. She earned many honors, including honorary doctoral degrees, prestigious awards, distinguished appointments, and dedications of schools and cultural centers in her name. In particular, she was named Poet Laureate of Illinois after the death of Carl Sandburg in 1967; the poetry consultant to the Library of Congress in 1985–1986; and the Jefferson Lecturer, the highest award in the humanities given by the federal government, in 1994. Tirelessly dedicated to art and humanity, she was especially committed to the encouragement of children and the support of the family until her death in her home on Chicago's South Side on December 3, 2000.

HIGHLIGHTS IN BROOK'S LIFE

1917	Gwendolyn Brooks is born in Topeka, Kansas, on June 7, and later moves with family to Chicago, Illinois.
1930	Publishes her first poem in *American Childhood*.
1933	Meets James Weldon Johnson and Langston Hughes.
1934	Graduates from Englewood High School; joins staff of the *Chicago Defender* and publishes in its weekly poetry column.
1936	Graduates from Wilson Junior College.
1939	Marries Henry Lowington Blakely II.
1940	Son, Henry Blakely, Jr., is born.
1941	Brooks attends writing class taught by Inez Cunningham Stark and reads widely in modern poetry.
1943	Wins poetry award from Midwestern Writers' Conference in Chicago.
1945	Publishes first collection of poems, *A Street in Bronzeville*; is selected by *Mademoiselle* as one of the magazine's "Ten Young Women of the Year."
1946	Brooks is awarded a Guggenheim Fellowship; becomes a fellow of the American Academy of Arts and Letters.
1947	Brooks is awarded a second Guggenheim Fellowship.
1948	Writes reviews for Chicago newspapers.
1950	Becomes the first African American to win a Pulitzer Prize, for *Annie Allen*.
1951	Daughter, Nora, is born.
1962	At the invitation of President John F. Kennedy, Brooks reads poetry at Library of Congress poetry festival.
1963	Begins first teaching job at Chicago's Columbia College.
1964	Receives honorary doctorate from Columbia College.
1967	Attends Black Writers' Conference at Fisk University in Nashville, Tennessee; teaches full-time at Chicago Teachers' College, North.
1968	Brooks is named Poet Laureate of Illinois.
1969	Separates from husband.
1971	Suffers mild heart attack on Christmas day; decides to discontinue teaching; travels to East Africa.
1974	Reconciles with husband.
1985	Serves as poetry consultant to Library of Congress.
1994	Brooks is selected as Jefferson Lecturer by the National Endowment for the Humanities.
2000	Dies of cancer in her Chicago home.

The Writer's Work

Although Gwendolyn Brooks has written autobiography, autobiographical fiction, children's literature, and articles for magazines, she is known primarily for her numerous collections of poetry. The most conspicuous qualities of her poetry are her sophisticated experiments in the forms of the ballad, sonnet, and mock epic; the depth of reading and the knowledge of tradition that underlie her writing; and her appreciation of the intrinsic beauty in ordinary people, things, and events.

Issues in Brooks's Poetry.

Brooks urges her readers to recognize that beauty goes beyond standard definitions and, in particular, that beauty is not a function of the color of one's skin. Brooks herself grew up on Chicago's South Side without the comforts and pleasures that wealth affords. Nevertheless, her family was unified by a strong bond of love and a sharing of simple pleasures. These satisfactions in family life are, for Brooks, substantive examples of beauty that surpass the superficial attractiveness of a shiny car or elegant clothing.

According to Brooks, conventional standards of beauty among human beings must be reevaluated. Elements of beauty may be defined by fashion magazines and television as light skin and a slender nose, but for Brooks these preferences are arbitrary. Brooks also explores the struggle to establish human freedom and to overcome oppression and hatred. She identifies those who hate and torment others because of their race, paying special attention to the seemingly normal lives of racists when they are not engaged in oppressive activities. She uncovers the wickedness of those who torture and murder children and shows the devastating effects on the victims of hatred. In the later period of her writing, she speaks to an African American audience, supporting in a literary and cultural sense the establishment of an African American nationality.

People in Brooks's Poetry.

Brooks focuses on urban life, especially the poor residents of the African American community. Her examination of these individuals reveals variety, humor, suffering, and personal dignity. The prevailing view is that poverty does not necessarily deny resourcefulness, creativity, and beauty to people. In contrast to the various residents of Bronzeville, Brooks also presents hypocritical people who presume to understand Bronzeville or who have a shallow sense of charity toward those living in poverty. Brooks describes the clothing, homes, language, frustrations, foibles, and dreams of her characters.

Beauty in the Ordinary.

Perhaps the most prevalent idea in all of Brooks's work is that "what was common was also a flower." Brooks strives to show that daily and ordinary things are too often overlooked and unappreciated even though they are worthy of respect and admiration. While visiting the White House, she noticed that the furnishings were dusted and polished and that the president's white shirt was especially white. However, for Brooks the beauty in the setting was not in the furnishings or the shirt but in her awareness of the numerous simple people who dedicated themselves to the careful preparations. Even though these workers were not present, their beauty was evident.

Brooks's Literary Importance.

During Brooks's career, some have charged that although her subject matter is black, her writing style is white. Others have charged that Brooks has benefited from white society's award structure and publishing industry without giving full recognition to her responsibility to the black community. To counter these objections, one should note that, regardless of her style or subject matter, Brooks has often been excluded from college curricula and literary anthologies; in addition, following her transformation at Fisk University in 1967, she showed full commitment to African

Photographer Wayne F. Miller captured these scenes of Chicago's South Side in the late 1940s. The tenements (bottom), photographed in 1946, were home to half of the city's black children. A woman takes a break from her sweeping while a boy delivers groceries in 1947 (top left), and a squatter is photographed in front of her shack on a cold winter day in 1948 (top right). Brooks lived and died on the South Side, and her writing reflects her love for its people.

SOME INSPIRATIONS BEHIND BROOK'S WORK

All authors are motivated by the people, places, and experiences that help to shape them. In the case of Gwendolyn Brooks, her parents were a central influence. Brooks's mother encouraged Brooks to write, and Brooks's father always sang for his children, creating a lasting impression of the connection between words and music. Brooks's father also supplied his daughter with a writing desk, so that she could properly apply herself to writing.

Brooks's experience in Chicago helped her to understand the complexities of racial relations. To complete her high-school education, she attended the predominantly white Hyde Park High School, the all-black Wendell Phillips High School, and the integrated Englewood High School. These changes in school populations enriched Brooks's outlook. Later, when Brooks and her husband moved into a kitchenette apartment in Chicago, the window overlooking the street became a great source of inspiration to Brooks, as the daily activities of the community provided endless ideas for her writing. Brooks has been inspired by her interest in children, drawing energy from eager young writers and helping them to take advantage of their talents.

Numerous people recognized Brooks's potential and encouraged her to write. The well-known authors James Weldon Johnson and Langston Hughes read her work and urged her to read widely and continue to write. Inez Cunningham Stark, who led a workshop for writers, made constructive remarks about her students' work, and Brooks learned to revise meticulously. At parties and social gatherings, Brooks met numerous young artists with whom she exchanged ideas. At a conference for black writers at Fisk University in 1967, the influence of Amiri Baraka helped Brooks to discover a role as a black writer with a black audience. Since that time, Brooks contributed extensively to the development of small, black-owned presses.

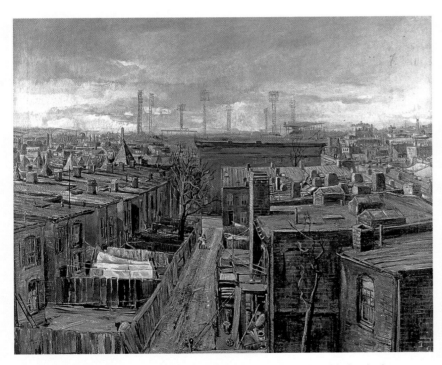

The Couple, a 1947 oil painting by John Farrar, reflects the humble beginning Brooks shared with her husband in a Chicago kitchenette apartment during the early years of their marriage. The daily activities Brooks observed from the apartment window gave birth to many writing ideas.

LONG FICTION

1953   Maud Martha

NONFICTION

1972   Report from Part One: An Autobiography
1975   A Capsule Course in Black Poetry Writing
1980   Young Poets' Primer
1996   Report from Part Two

POETRY

1945   A Street in Bronzeville
1949   Annie Allen
1960   The Bean Eaters
1963   Selected Poems
1966   We Real Cool
1967   The Wall
1968   In the Mecca
1969   Riot
1970   Family Pictures
1971   Aloneness
1971   Black Steel: Joe Frazier and Muhammad Ali
1972   Aurora
1975   Beckonings
1980   Primer for Blacks
1981   To Disembark
1982   Black Love
1986   The Near-Johannesburg Boy
1987   Blacks
1988   Gottschalk and the Grande Tarantelle
1988   Winnie
1991   Children Coming Home

CHILDREN'S LITERATURE

1956   Bronzeville Boys and Girls
1974   The Tiger Who Wore White Gloves: Or, You Are What You Are
1983   Very Young Poets

EDITED TEXT

1971   Jump Bad: A New Chicago Anthology

MISCELLANEOUS

1971   The World of Gwendolyn Brooks

American readers and independent publishers. She is what the African American author Haki Madhubuti calls "a national treasure," because she retains all of her personal and cultural heritage and makes it a source of inspiration for all Americans, especially children.

BIBLIOGRAPHY

Bloom, Harold, ed. *Modern Critical Views: Gwendolyn Brooks*. Philadelphia: Chelsea House, 2000.

Bolden, B. J. *Urban Rage in Bronzeville: Social Commentary in the Poetry of Gwendolyn Brooks, 1945–1960*. Chicago: Third World Press, 1999.

Clarke, Cheryl. "The Loss of Lyric Space." *Kenyon Review* 17 (1995): 136–147.

Kent, George E. *A Life of Gwendolyn Brooks*. Lexington: University Press of Kentucky, 1990.

Melhem, D. H. *Gwendolyn Brooks: Poetry and the Heroic Voice*. Lexington: University Press of Kentucky, 1987.

Mootry, Maria K., and Gary Smith, eds. *A Life Distilled: Gwendolyn Brooks, Her Poetry and Fiction*. Urbana: University of Illinois Press, 1987.

Parisi, Joseph. *Poets in Person: A Listener's Guide*. 2d ed. Chicago: Poetry Press, 1997.

Schweik, Susan M. "The Masculine V-letter—(Not) Playing with Mimesis: Gwendolyn Brooks and the Stuff of Letters." In *American Women Poets and the Second World War*. Madison: University of Wisconsin Press, 1991.

Stanford, Ann Folwell. "An Epic with a Difference: Sexual Politics in Gwendolyn Brooks's 'The Anniad.'" *American Literature* 67 (1995): 283–301.

Walker, Margaret Alexander, and Joanne V. Gabbin. "Blooming in the Whirlwind: The Early Poetry of Gwendolyn Brooks." In *The Furious Flowering of African-American Poetry*, edited by Joanne V. Gabbin. Charlottesville: University Press of Virginia, 1999.

Reader's Guide to Major Works

ANNIE ALLEN

   Genre: Poetry
   Subgenre: Coming-of-age story
   Published: New York, 1949
   Time period: 1940s
   Setting: Fictitious community of
    Bronzeville

Themes and Issues. *Annie Allen* is, on one hand, a challenging sequence of poems because of its sophisticated style, elevated language, and complex references. On the other hand, the work is also a universally accessible story of Annie's maturation and her relationship with her parents, friends, and husband.

The Poems. In "the ballad of late Annie" one sees the conflict between Annie and her mother as well as Annie's pickiness about a suitor. Annie lies in "her bower," feeling very attractive, but her mother insists that Annie either take up "a broom to whish the doors / Or get a man to marry." The "proud late Annie" has high standards for any man who might qualify to marry her. Such a man must offer the finery of lacquer, pearls, and opals if he is to be worthy of her. Implicit in the poem is the idea that Annie's standards are too high and the reality that she will have to lower her expectations.

In "The Anniad," one finds one of Gwendolyn Brooks's most difficult works. The title is a combination of the name of the collection's title character and the titles of classical works such as Homer's *Iliad* (c. 800 B.C.E.) and Virgil's *Aeneid* (c. 29–19 B.C.E.). Like *The Rape of the Lock* by Alexander Pope, "The Anniad" is a mock epic: The poem uses an exalted style and design to render a story that is low and com-

mon, at first for a comical effect, but in the end for a sorrowful effect.

Instead of presenting a great man on a glorious quest, Brooks describes a black girl and her love relationship. Annie's lover is Tan Man, who loves her in "a lowly room. Which she makes a chapel of." Tan Man, like a knight in Annie's dreams, goes off to war but, on his return, slips into unfaithfulness. Annie's fantasy of exalted love finally exists only in her memory.

The concluding portion of *Annie Allen* is a sequence titled "The Womanhood." In this sequence, a poem given only "II" as a title discusses the life of Annie's child, whose fearlessness and ceaseless "reaching," despite disruptions and injuries, are the pride of the mother. In "the rites for Cousin Vit," tribute is paid to a deceased woman who found such pleasure in the mild vices of her life that even in death she is not dead: She surely rises from

The passion of Annie Allen's love relationship with Tan Man is reflected in Michael Escoffery's 1996 painting *Moonlight Lovers*. Although Tan Man actually loves Annie in "a lowly room," Annie's perspective glorifies the setting and Tan Man's devotion to her. *Annie Allen*, Brooks's 1949 book of poetry, won Brooks the Pulitzer Prize in Poetry. Brooks was the first African American to win a Pulitzer Prize.

the coffin that cannot hold her and resumes her "haply hysterics."

In "I love those little booths at Benvenuti's," Brooks satirizes visitors to a restaurant frequented mostly by blacks. The white visitors hope to get an insider's perspective on black culture and style, but the "colored people will not 'clown.'" The visitors are left to wonder "how shall they tell people they have been / Out Bronzeville way," but their visit leaves them uninformed.

Analysis. *Annie Allen* intensified Brooks's focus on women's issues, building upon the themes of sexual politics and female resistance to passivity and male oppression that are present in *A Street in Bronzeville*. Perhaps Brooks's greatest technical achievement, *Annie Allen*, which won the Pulitzer Prize in 1950, marks her advancement to a poet of enduring national fame.

SOURCES FOR FURTHER STUDY

Kunitz, Stanley. "Bronze by Gold." In *On Gwendolyn Brooks: Reliant Contemplation*, edited by Stephen Caldwell Wright. Ann Arbor: University of Michigan Press, 1996.

Stanford, Ann Folwell. "An Epic with a Difference: Sexual Politics in Gwendolyn Brooks's 'The Anniad.'" *American Literature* 67 (1995): 283–301.

Tate, Claudia. "Anger So Flat: Gwendolyn Brooks's *Annie Allen*." In *Modern Critical Views: Gwendolyn Brooks*, edited by Harold Bloom. Philadelphia: Chelsea House, 2000.

A STREET IN BRONZEVILLE
   Genre: Poetry
   Subgenre: Social commentary
   Published: New York, 1945
   Time period: 1940s
   Setting: Fictitious community based on
   Chicago's South Side

Themes and Issues. This collection of poems examines the citizens and social conditions of Bronzeville, a fictitious but realistic African American community.

The Poems. In "the mother," Brooks creates an enduring dramatic monologue that reveals the anxiety of a woman who has given birth to some children but has chosen to abort other pregnancies. The speaker is a loving mother who is familiar with all the joys and trials of raising children, yet she is haunted by the spirits of the unborn children of her terminated pregnancies. She fumbles with words to justify or excuse her actions but can find satisfaction only in her determined declaration that she loved all the children she conceived. Brooks notes that she is not taking sides on the issue of abortion; instead, she is exploring how motherhood and abortion fill the mind of a particular woman.

In "obituary for a living lady," Brooks is more descriptive than dramatic. The speaker is apparently a citizen in Bronzeville, but not much is revealed about her, except that she has a friend who is very reserved about sexual contact. This friend loved a man but would not permit the slightest sexual advances. As a result, the courtship cooled, and the man pursued "a woman who dressed in red." Even though the speaker's friend "decided that the next time she would say 'yes,'" the opportunity was already lost. Now the speaker's friend continues her reserved lifestyle, never dancing and refusing to wear perfume or lipstick. Although she is naturally beautiful, she resigns herself to the love of religion. At her church, the preacher finds her attractive, but her steadfast attitude about sex looms as an inevitable barrier to any fulfillment. Brooks's title implies that the friend's reserved attitude is actually a refusal to live—because the woman cannot frankly face sexuality, she is not truly alive.

Like "obituary for a living lady," "The Sundays of Satin Legs Smith" is more descriptive than dramatic. Brooks softly satirizes Satin Legs, who thinks of himself as a king: Brooks declares that lovers have given him his "title," that at the start of his day he is "royal," and that he plans his day as a "reign." Nevertheless, the wardrobe of this king is full of gaudy clothing, including "wonder-suits in yellow and in wine" and "hats / Like bright umbrellas." This laughably royal figure is part of Bronzeville, but Satin Legs "hears and does not hear" the mundane sounds that surround him. He "sees and does not see" the broken windows, patched clothing, and hungry people in his neighborhood.

William H. Johnson's male subject in his painting *Jitterbugs* (Smithsonian American Art Museum, Washington, D.C.) embodies all the gaudy charm of Brooks's character Satin Legs Smith, one of the inhabitants of the fictitious community of Bronzeville in Brooks's first book of poetry, *A Street in Bronzeville*.

Legs, Brooks makes recurring references to "you," presumably her reader. "You" cannot fully know the southern heritage of Satin Legs. His satisfactions in dress, entertainment, food, and female companionship are beyond anything "you" might ever really experience.

Analysis. While some of the poems in *A Street in Bronzeville* are ballads or sonnets, Brooks also works out subtle variations on these forms. The language is sometimes as elevated as the idiom of the modernists, but at other times it is direct, frank, and idiomatic. The poems in this volume reflect a voice of resistance to the racism of the United States. Brooks portrays the lives of urban blacks in attentive detail and modernist tones.

SOURCES FOR FURTHER STUDY

Bolden, Barbara Jean. *Urban Rage in Bronzeville: Social Commentary in the Poetry of Gwendolyn Brooks*. Chicago: Third World Press, 1999.

Callahan, John F. "Essentially an Essential African: Gwendolyn Brooks and the Awakening to Audience." *North Dakota Quarterly* 55, no. 4 (1987): 59–73.

Smith, Gary. "Gwendolyn Brooks's *A Street in Bronzeville*, the Harlem Renaissance, and the Mythologies of Black Women." In *Modern Critical Views: Gwendolyn Brooks*, edited by Harold Bloom. Philadelphia: Chelsea House, 2000.

Despite these realities, Satin Legs takes "his lady" to dinner, and she, dressed in "Queen lace stockings," helps him maintain his air of royalty. In addition to this description of Satin

Other Works

THE BEAN EATERS (1960). This poetry collection continues Gwendolyn Brooks's examination of the Bronzeville community but goes on to interpret incidents in the struggle for civil rights. The collection's title poem honors "an old yellow pair." Because of poverty, these folks live in a back room and eat beans, not meat, but they are "mostly good" and are honorably humble. In contrast, the poem "We Real Cool" is an ironic presentation of local pool players who find excitement in quitting school, drinking, and carousing, but the final line insists that they are only choosing death.

Going beyond these studies of Bronzeville, Brooks offers "A Bronzeville Mother Loiters in Mississippi. Meanwhile, a Mississippi Mother Burns Bacon." The poem is a study of the murderer of Emmett Till, "a blackish child / Of fourteen" who was tortured, murdered, and cast into a river because he allegedly whistled or said something suggestive to a white woman. The murderer, described as "the Fine Prince," is back at home after being declared innocent in a Mississippi court. The murderer's wife, who was the victim of the "Dark Villain," prepares a breakfast for her babies and her husband, but when the babies misbehave, the "Fine Prince" slaps one child viciously. The wife is frightened by the violence, and when the husband tries to soothe her, she is repulsed and horrified.

FAMILY PICTURES (1970). This collection of poetry presents a series of young heroes. Perhaps the most notable is described in "The Life of Lincoln West." Young Lincoln, by ordinary standards, is not an attractive child, but he has a sweet heart and a desire to please others and to be accepted. When a racist in a movie theater regards Lincoln as "the / real thing," a clear representative "of the specie," Lincoln's mother is offended, and she confronts the racist and angrily leaves the theater. The irony, however, is that Lincoln himself, after relentless abuse in his life, savors the phrase "the real thing." Whenever he is hurt or troubled, he brings the phrase up in his heart to comfort himself.

Also in this collection is "Paul Robeson," a poem in tribute to the extraordinary African American scholar, athlete, actor, singer, and expatriate. Robeson, according to Brooks, warns "in music-words / devout and large / that we are each other's / harvest."

MAUD MARTHA (1953). This, Brooks's only novel, is an autobiographical fiction that renders in clear prose the themes that some readers find difficult to understand in Brooks's poetry. Brooks analyzes what people perceive as beauty, noting their preference for light skin. She reveals the diversity among her neighbors in the black community and shows the complexities of courtship, marriage, and parenthood. Despite the frustrations of racism, Maud Martha, the book's central character, steadily matures and develops a positive outlook.

Readers of *A Street in Bronzeville* will enjoy the chapter "kitchenette folks," which describes the residents of "Gappington Arms," an apartment building that houses diverse citizens. One meets Oberto, who loves his sexy wife; Clement Lewy, who loves his mother even though she leaves him to fend for himself while she goes to

John Biggers's pencil-on-paper illustration *Sharecroppers* captures the poverty of "an old yellow pair" in Brooks's poem "The Bean Eaters" as well as the companionship of Mr. and Mrs. Whitestripe, residents of "Gappington Arms" in Brooks's only novel, *Maud Martha*.

work; Maryginia Washington, who asserts that she is a descendant of George Washington; and Mr. and Mrs. Whitestripe, who love each other tenderly, even in their old age.

Readers of *Annie Allen* will enjoy *Maud Martha* for its clear description of the maturation of a young black woman and her transformation from childhood to adolescence, marriage, and motherhood. Maud's difficulties with her husband, Paul, correspond to the difficulties of Annie with Tan Man in "The Anniad."

REPORT FROM PART ONE: AN AUTOBIOGRAPHY (1972). This collection of introductory tributes, personal memories, numerous photos, and several interviews reveals the life of Gwendolyn Brooks. The book is a valuable resource for those seeking added insight into Brooks's heritage, intellectual development, teaching experience, and writings. The book, noteworthy as a publication of Dudley Randall's Broadside Press, is a key step in Brooks's moving away from mainstream publishers to work with independent black presses.

A chapter titled "Report from Part One," which originally appeared in *McCall's*, describes Brooks's family tree and reveals aspects of the warm and pleasant home life Brooks enjoyed, especially her family's holiday celebrations and traditional feasts. Brooks also recounts her adolescent experiences, her early years of marriage, and her literary activities with her husband at the workshop of Inez Cunningham Stark and at various parties that gathered artists from the community. Brooks chronicles her literary development, including her work as a reviewer, a teacher, and a participant at the Fisk University Writers' Conference in 1967. Ending her "report" with characteristic modesty, Brooks says she feels "qualified to enter at least the kindergarten of the new consciousness."

In the chapter "African Fragment," Brooks provides a diary of her visit to Nairobi, Kenya, and Dar es Salaam, Tanzania. She describes her fascination with the geography, the development of cities, and the special people she met, including Margaret Kenyatta, the daughter of Kenya's first president, Jomo Kenyatta, and novelist Ayi Kwei Armah. She concludes the diary with a warning: "Don't come over, Afro-Americans, expecting everything to move as it does in the United States."

The final sections of *Report from Part One* serve as a compact source for clarifications about Brooks's life and work. Several interviews address Brooks's practices as a writer, her views on civil rights, and her intentions in various poems. A section titled "Sources and Illuminations" presents notes and comments on individual writings.

Resources

The papers of Gwendolyn Brooks are housed at Atlanta University in Atlanta, Georgia.

Audio Recordings. Many audio recordings are available featuring the work or commentary of Gwendolyn Brooks. *Gwendolyn Brooks Reading Her Poetry* (1973) includes poems from *A Street in Bronzeville, Annie Allen, The Bean Eaters,* and *Selected Poems*. Don L. Lee (Haki Madhubuti) reads an introductory poem entitled "Gwendolyn Brooks" and provides notes that are included in the tape package. *A Gwendolyn Brooks Treasury: A Pulitzer Prize Laureate Discusses Poverty and Solitude* (1969) features Gwendolyn Brooks reading from her own works, revealing the poverty and solitude of blacks in the United States. *Lucille Clifton and Gwendolyn Brooks* (1996) is a recording of the two poets reading their poems before an audience at the Solomon R. Guggenheim Museum on May 3, 1983. *Poets in Person* (1992) is a set of seven cassettes that includes a listener's guide and features a conversation between Gwendolyn Brooks and Alice Fulton.

Video Recordings. *Not a Rhyme Time* (1999), produced by PBS, is volume 5 in the series *I'll Make Me a World*. In this program, Brooks comments on her career and the transformation she underwent following the conference at Fisk University in 1967. Another video, *A Conversation with Gwendolyn Brooks* (1989), features an interview of Brooks by Alan Jabbour and E. Ethelbert Miller as Brooks completes her term as twenty-ninth poetry consultant to the Library of Congress for 1985–1986. The conversation includes comments on the poet's early life, her influences and family life, and her contributions to American letters.

Poetry in Motion. This collection of forty-six broadside subway posters was produced in 1996 for the New York City Transit Authority/Metropolitan Transportation Authority and includes work by Gwendolyn Brooks. The multicolored posters are printed on glossy card stock; the upper border on each broadside has the poem's title and a reproduction of decorations from a New York subway station.

WILLIAM T. LAWLOR

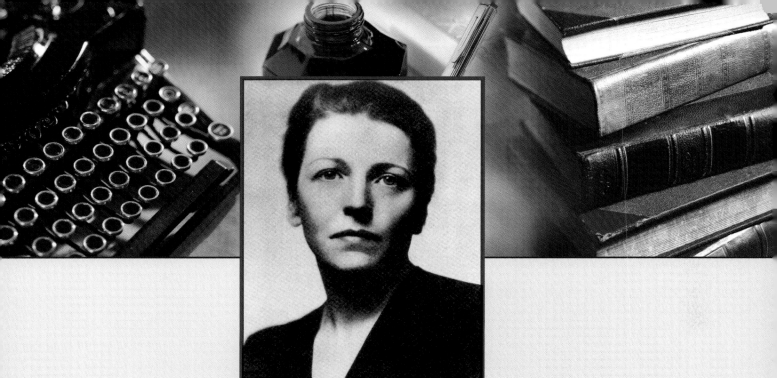

Pearl S. Buck

BORN: June 26, 1892, Hillsboro, West Virginia
DIED: March 6, 1973, Danby, Vermont
IDENTIFICATION: Mid-twentieth-century novelist associated with China and the United States, known for her books explaining China to the West.

The author of more than seventy published books, Pearl S. Buck is the most translated of all American writers. After winning a Pulitzer Prize, she became the first American woman to win a Nobel Prize. Her most admired fiction treats Chinese culture and history and serves to introduce Asia to the average Westerner. Buck's personal influence helped to establish relations between China and the United States. On the domestic scene, she addressed meetings, raised funds, and contributed large amounts of her own money to advance the causes of civil rights and women's rights. She also worked extensively on behalf of mentally disabled children, orphans, and neglected children of American Asian parents.

Pearl S. Buck was born Pearl Comfort Sydenstricker in Hillsboro, West Virginia, on June 26, 1892. She was the fifth child of a Protestant missionary couple, Absalom and Carie Stulting Sydenstricker. Three months later her parents brought her to China, where she grew up bilingual and fully versed in Chinese customs and attitudes. She had almost no conception of American life until the summer of 1901, when the Sydenstrickers returned to West Virginia on a year's furlough.

Once back in China, Buck absorbed colloquial Chinese from her governess (*amah*) and studied the classics more formally with a male tutor. Her mother supplied her with miscellaneous reading material in English, but she acquired little but biblical lore from her father, a rigid fundamentalist Christian. The echoes of scriptural cadences and rhetoric helped to impart a flowing and familiar tone to her early fiction. Close contact with the Chinese people, especially those of the lower classes, formed the basis of Buck's later identification with the oppressed of all races. At sixteen she volunteered at Shanghai shelters for abandoned slaves and prostitutes, teaching sewing and other domestic activities.

International Education. In the fall of 1910 Buck enrolled at Randolph-Macon Woman's College in Lynchburg, Virginia, where she contributed poems and stories to the undergraduate literary magazine and was president of her class. She graduated in 1914, and in 1916 she met a young agricultural missionary, John Lossing Buck, whom she married a year later.

The Sydenstricker family home in Hillsboro, West Virginia, the birthplace of Pearl Buck.

The Sydenstricker family in about 1900. From left to right are Pearl, Absalom, Grace, and Carie. Behind them stands Wang Amah, the children's governess.

The Bucks' union was based largely on a common religious background and their mutual interest in Chinese culture. Both were endowed, moreover, with high intelligence, industry, and dedication. John Buck in his own field eventually obtained almost as much recognition as his wife did in hers. However, he never treated Buck as an equal, only as a homemaker, mother, and helper in his own work. Although the marriage lasted for eighteen years, it was unsuccessful. For two years the Bucks lived in a Chinese farming community, from which Pearl imbibed much of the background for her masterpiece *The Good Earth* (1931). In 1919 Pearl accepted a faculty position at Nanking University, and Pearl taught English there on a part-time basis.

Domestic Life. Shortly after giving birth to a daughter, Carol Grace, in March 1920, Buck was informed that the child had a tumor requiring treatment in the United States. At this time, Buck was told that she would be unable to bear any more children. In the next year, soon after returning to China, Buck received another blow when her mother died. She also began to realize that her daughter was mentally impaired beyond the hope of cure. In the summer of 1924 Buck and her husband registered for graduate work at Cornell University, where Buck wrote a prizewinning essay on the topic for which she would become most known, "China and the West." Buck's master's thesis, however, covered a conventional topic, a survey of the personal essay from the sixteenth to the twentieth century.

Life in China. Buck's first professionally published work, "In China, Too," appeared in the *Atlantic Monthly* in January 1924. The article compared the dramatic social changes taking place in China with those in the rest of the world, especially in regard to the status of women. During an armed conflict between nationalist troops and those of independent warlords, the Bucks' house was looted while they hid in the quarters of a servant. They were rescued by American soldiers and retired to a small Japanese city near Nagasaki, returning to Shanghai in October 1927. In the summer of 1928 the family returned briefly to New York City, where John had been awarded a sizable grant. Buck entered her daughter in a boarding facility in New Jersey. On a visit to

HIGHLIGHTS IN BUCK'S LIFE

1892 Pearl S. Buck is born Pearl Comfort Sydenstricker on June 26 in Hillsboro, West Virginia; is later brought by missionary parents to China.

1908 Volunteers in Shanghai shelters for female slaves and prostitutes.

1910 Enrolls at Randolph-Macon Woman's College in Lynchburg, Virginia.

1914 Graduates in June; accepts teaching post at a missionary college in Shanghai.

1916 Meets agricultural missionary John Lossing Buck, whom she marries the following spring.

1919 Moves with husband to Nanking and teaches in the university.

1920 Gives birth to a daughter, Carol Grace, later discovered to be mentally disabled.

1924 Publishes first professional work, "In China, Too," in *Atlantic Monthly*; begins graduate study at Cornell University; adopts a three-year-old girl.

1925 Writes prizewinning essay "China and the West."

1926 Publishes first short story, "A Chinese Woman Speaks," in *Asia*; returns to Nanking.

1927 Takes refuge in Unzen, Japan, during internal hostilities in China.

1928 Visits New York City with John Lossing Buck.

1930 Returns to Nanking; finishes writing *The Good Earth*.

1931 Publishes *The Good Earth*.

1932 Is awarded Pulitzer Prize for *The Good Earth*; returns to United States.

1933 Publishes *All Men Are Brothers*.

1935 Divorces John Lossing Buck and marries Richard J. Walsh.

1938 Publishes *This Proud Heart*; is awarded Nobel Prize in Literature.

1941 Establishes East and West Association; publishes *Of Men and Women*.

1945 Publishes *The Townsman* under pseudonym John Sedges.

1949 Establishes adoption agency, Welcome House, especially for mixed race and minority children.

1963 Begins relationship with ballroom dance instructor Theodore Harris, which continues until her death.

1973 Dies in Danby, Vermont, of lung cancer; is inducted into National Women's Hall of Fame.

contemporary classics

THE
GOOD EARTH
PEARL S. BUCK

The Classic Novel of Pre-revolutionary China
by the Nobel Prize-winning Author

FEATURING A READING GROUP GUIDE

the John Day publishing company, which had accepted her first novel, *East Wind: West Wind* (1930), Buck met its president, Richard Walsh, who became her lover and eventually her second husband.

Miracle Years. In May 1930 Buck completed writing her best-selling masterpiece, *The Good Earth*, which was published the following year. Conventional in style and technique but new and startling in subject matter, it immediately brought Buck worldwide acclaim, as well as a Pulitzer Prize and the William Dean Howells Medal from the American Academy of Arts and Letters. The theme of an underprivileged farmer whose heroic efforts enable him to buy much of the surrounding land on which he toils had nothing in common with popular fiction of the day. The farmer's painful but steady struggle ends as much in spiritual satisfaction as in material reward.

Buck almost concurrently worked in another literary genre, translating a traditional Chinese historical novel to which she gave the title *All Men Are Brothers* (1933). Its more than one thousand pages celebrate the exploits of a group of outlaws who resemble the English Robin Hood and his band of thieves. As in *The Good Earth*, the narrative reveals Buck's affiliation with the land and the common people as well as her understanding of Chinese language and culture.

American Themes. In November 1932 Buck addressed a luncheon for Presbyterian women on the topic "Is There a Case for Foreign Missions?" She answered in the negative, and,

King Gustav V of Sweden presents Buck with the Nobel Prize for Literature on December 21, 1938, in Stockholm, Sweden.

not surprisingly, she resigned from her own position in the missionary six months later. As a result, some conservative religious circles regarded Buck unfavorably, disapproving even more in the following year, when she sued for divorce. Buck's novel *This Proud Heart* (1938) loosely parallels her own domestic situation but is set in the urban United States. The protagonist, a young female sculptor, is trapped in an unhappy marriage to a husband who expects her to play the traditional role of mother and homemaker and discourages her career.

Buck wrote five novels under the pseudonym John Sedges, doing so, she explained, "because men have fewer handicaps in our society than women have, in writing as well as in other professions." It was also the case that Buck was known primarily for her works about China and she wanted to test her ability to portray life in small-town America. In *The Townsman* (1945) she praised country life in the Midwest. In a similarly optimistic vein, she published *Portrait of a Marriage* (1945), in which a wealthy artist and an uneducated farm woman find happiness together despite their presumably incompatible backgrounds. *The Hidden Flower* (1952) describes the completely opposite consequences of a biracial marriage between a Japanese woman and an American Army officer.

Buck was made a member of the National Institute of Arts and Letters in 1936, and in 1951 she was elected to the American Academy of Arts and Letters. She is pictured above at a press conference at the Foundation of Modern Arts on January 28, 1965.

War Years and After.

At the outset of World War II, Buck was at first ambivalent about U.S. participation. She engaged actively, however, in fundraising for China's struggle against Japan, sponsoring the China Emergency Relief Committee and other organizations. In the March 1, 1941, issue of the magazine *Asia*, she issued a "Warning to Free Nations," calling for guaranteed equal rights to oppressed groups, including Chinese peasants, black Americans, and the entire nation of India. In 1941 she founded the East and West Association and served for many years as its president. In 1942 she chaired a national Committee Against Racial Discrimination. Subsequently she wrote in favor of an early version of the Equal Rights Amendment for women, spoke out against the Chinese Exclusion Acts, and served as co-president of the India League of America.

In 1960 Buck returned to Japan to supervise the filming of her children's book *The Big Wave*, which had been published in 1948. She also visited Korea, where she was overwhelmed by the suffering of mixed-race children. She tried to educate the American public about the plight of the Korean people in a historical novel, *The Living Reed* (1963). Following the death of her second husband in 1960, Buck entrusted both her professional and private destinies to Theodore Harris, a ballroom dance instructor, forty years her junior, whom she had hired for her children. Harris remained with her until her death in 1973. In 1964 she established, with a one-million-dollar donation, the Pearl S. Buck Foundation to assist Asian children fathered by American servicemen. Buck kept up both her humanitarian and her literary work until her death, a living example of determination, energy, and pride.

The Writer's Work

Although Pearl S. Buck wrote in nearly every prose genre, she is chiefly famous for her long fiction, most of which concerns contemporary issues in East Asia and the United States. Her universal themes encompass love, marriage, the family, economic strife, and war. Her characters resemble ordinary people in realistic environments, whether they are empresses or peasant farmers. Nearly all her works reflect her deeply held social and political ideals. She consistently contrasts East and West, tradition and reform, and patriarchy and equality in gender relationships.

Resourceful Women and Motley Men.

Buck's women are uniformly good, but her men are both good and bad. Even the Empress Dowager Zi-Xi in *Imperial Woman* (1956) is described as "generous and kind." Buck wrote twin biographies of her mother, *The Exile* (1936), and her father, *Fighting Angel: Portrait of a Soul* (1936). She sympathetically portrays her mother as a victim of her status as a missionary wife but paints her father less sympathetically as intolerant in his beliefs and behavior. The protagonist of *The Good Earth* is far from exemplary, but the hero of *The Townsman* is a stalwart character. There is little to be admired in the protagonist of *Other Gods: An American Legend* (1940), a celebrated American mountain climber whose rise to fame depends largely on public relations techniques. *Kinfolk* (1949) criticizes a Chinese expatriate who lives in luxury in Manhattan on the proceeds of his books expounding Chinese culture to the West while he remains indifferent to suffering in his native land. The two main characters of *God's Men* (1951) are closely involved with war-torn China. One altruistically devotes his energies to providing food and other relief for the needy, while the other cares only about building a journalistic empire.

Women's Issues.

Buck first based her treatment of the social disadvantages of women upon conditions in China but gradually came to use China as a symbol of the United States. Her first published work of fiction, "A Chinese Woman Speaks," contrasts the traditional marital relationship in which men are more powerful with the modern enlightened condition of uniform equality. In *The Good Earth*, the slave O-Lan performs with heroic fortitude the conventionally servile roles of wife, daughter-in-law, and mother. The story "The First Wife" (1933) contrasts these conventional roles with those of the modern emancipated woman. In *The Mother* (1934), the protagonist, a farmer's wife deserted by her husband, is sexually frustrated and tormented by loneliness.

In *This Proud Heart*, Buck changes locale from China to the United States and atmosphere from despondency to triumph as the protagonist demonstrates that a woman's career is more valid and satisfying than marriage and domesticity. In *Pavilion of Women* (1946), it is the wife rather than the husband who rebels against the restrictions of matrimony. The biracial marriage in *The Hidden Flower* is threatened by racial prejudices rather than the husband's insensitivity.

Buck's Position in World Literature.

There is no question about Buck's universal popularity. She is the most widely translated of all American writers, and four of her novels were turned into films. She won a Nobel Prize in Literature, a Pulitzer Prize, and the William Dean Howells Medal for Distinguished Fiction. However, her critics and contemporaries tended to overlook the clarity, epic flow, and vivid characterization in her work. They found her perspectives too optimistic, her plots too facile, and her didacticism too obvious.

Buck did not follow the contemporary trend toward symbolism and stream-of-consciousness. By the end of the twentieth century, however, perhaps due to radically changing social and economic conditions, Buck was recognized as one of the major writers of her time. The tenacity of her opposition to marital, social, and political injustice met the strong approval of feminists and human-rights advocates. The advent of commercial globalization, moreover, had a strong effect upon the literary world, bringing about a new interest in literary relations between the East and the West.

Vita Petrosky Solomon's 1968 oil painting *Portrait of Pearl Buck* captures the quiet grace of a woman whose humanitarian efforts rival her accomplishments as a writer.

BIBLIOGRAPHY

Block, Irvin. *The Lives of Pearl Buck: A Tale of China and America*. New York: Crowell, 1973.

Conn, Peter. *Pearl S. Buck: A Cultural Biography*. New York: Cambridge University Press, 1996.

Doyle, Paul A. *Pearl S. Buck*. Rev. ed. Boston: Twayne Publishers, 1980.

Harris, Theodore F. *Pearl S. Buck*. 2 vols. New York: John Day, 1969.

Liao, Kang. *Pearl S. Buck: A Cultural Bridge Across the Pacific*. Westport, Conn.: Greenwood Press, 1997.

Lipscomb, Elizabeth J., Francis E. Webb, and Peter Conn, eds. *The Several Worlds of Pearl S. Buck: Essays Presented at a Centennial Symposium, Randolph-Macon Woman's College, March 26–28, 1992*. Westport, Conn.: Greenwood Press, 1992.

Rizzon, Beverly. *Pearl S. Buck: The Final Chapter*. Palm Springs, Calif.: ETC Publications, 1989.

Spenser, Cornelia. *The Exile's Daughter: A Biography of Pearl S. Buck*. New York: Coward-McCann, 1944.

Stirling, Nora B. *Pearl S. Buck: A Woman in Conflict*. Piscataway, N.J.: New Century Publishers, 1983.

Yu, Yuh-chao. *Pearl S. Buck's Fiction: A Cross-Cultural Interpretation*. Taipei, China: Academica Sinica, 1981.

FILMS BASED ON BUCK STORIES

1937 The Good Earth

1944 Dragon Seed

1945 China Sky

1960 The Big Wave

1962 Satan Never Sleeps

1965 The Guide

SOME INSPIRATIONS BEHIND BUCK'S WORK

In her earliest years Pearl S. Buck imbibed a love of Chinese culture, landscape, and art that permeates her major works. Her ten years spent in the Chinese countryside as the wife of an agricultural missionary familiarized her with the cruelties and humiliations of absolute poverty. Her masterpiece *The Good Earth* mirrors the struggles of farm life and pays tribute to the courage and determination of those who survive its rigors. *The Mother* depicts the same grim surroundings but concentrates on the loneliness and sexual frustrations of the farm wife. *Pavilion of Women* portrays a middle-class household in which the wife rebels against the Confucian tradition that ranks the father and sons ahead of the wife and mother. The extremes of wealth and power are revealed in *Imperial Woman*, a historical novel concerning the late nineteenth-century Empress Dowager Zi-Xi, who rose against tremendous odds from obscurity to a position of international eminence.

LONG FICTION

1930 East Wind: West Wind
1931 The Good Earth
1932 Sons
1934 The Mother
1935 A House Divided
1935 House of Earth
1938 This Proud Heart
1939 The Patriot
1940 Other Gods: An American Legend
1942 Dragon Seed
1942 China Sky
1943 The Promise
1945 China Flight
1945 Portrait of a Marriage
1945 The Townsman (as John Sedges)
1946 Pavilion of Women
1947 The Angry Wife (as Sedges)
1948 Peony
1949 Kinfolk
1949 The Long Love (as Sedges)
1951 God's Men
1952 The Hidden Flower
1952 Bright Procession (as Sedges)
1953 Come, My Beloved
1953 Voices in the House (as Sedges)
1956 Imperial Woman
1957 Letter from Peking
1959 Command the Morning
1962 Satan Never Sleeps
1963 The Living Reed
1965 Death in the Castle
1967 The Time Is Noon
1968 The New Year
1969 The Three Daughters of Madame Liang
1970 Mandala
1972 The Goddess Abides
1973 All Under Heaven
1974 The Rainbow

SHORT FICTION

1933 The First Wife and Other Stories
1941 Today and Forever
1943 Twenty-seven Stories
1947 Far and Near, Stories of Japan, China, and America
1962 Hearts Come Home and Other Stories
1969 The Good Deed and Other Stories
1972 Once upon a Christmas
1975 East and West
1976 Secrets of the Heart
1977 The Lovers and Other Stories
1979 The Woman Who Was Changed and Other Stories

NONFICTION

1932 East and West and the Novel
1936 The Exile
1936 Fighting Angel: Portrait of a Soul
1939 The Chinese Novel
1941 Of Men and Women (expanded 1971)
1942 American Unity and Asia
1943 What America Means to Me
1945 China in Black and White
1945 Talk About Russia: With Masha Scott
1945 Tell the People: Talks with James Yen About the Mass Education Movement
1947 How it Happens: Talk About the German People, 1914–1933, with Erna von Pustau

1949 American Argument: With Eslanda Goode Robeson
1950 The Child Who Never Grew
1954 Johnny Jack and His Beginnings
1954 My Several Worlds: A Personal Record
1958 Friend to Friend: A Candid Exchange Between Pearl S. Buck and Carlos F. Romulo
1962 A Bridge for Passing
1964 The Joy of Children
1965 Children for Adoption
1965 The Gifts They Bring: Our Debt to the Mentally Retarded
1966 The People of Japan
1967 To My Daughters with Love
1970 China as I See It
1970 The Kennedy Women: A Personal Appraisal
1971 The Story Bible
1971 Pearl S. Buck's America
1972 China Past and Present

CHILDREN'S LITERATURE

1932 The Young Revolutionist
1940 Stories for Little Children
1948 The Big Wave
1952 One Bright Day and Other Stories for Children
1953 The Man Who Changed China: The Story of Sun Yat-Sen
1961 Fourteen Stories

TRANSLATION

1933 All Men Are Brothers (of a novel attributed to Shih Nai-an)

Filming The Good Earth

Broadway producers were the first to recognize the dramatic possibilities in Wang Lung's domestic trials and triumphs. A production staged by the Theatre Guild opened in New York in October 1932. Despite a large cast dominated by Hollywood celebrities Claude Rains, Alla Nazimova, and Sydney Greenstreet, the play disappointed critics and public alike, closing after fifty-eight performances. The theater offered an excellent venue for reproducing the major characters' relationships, but it could not adequately assimilate the atmosphere of Asian culture, the sweep of the Chinese landscape, or the epic struggles of Wang and O-Lan. Although Buck was disappointed in the play's short run, she was, nevertheless, gratified that it had been produced. "The book I wrote has taken on a new life of its own," she remarked, "a life beyond my conception . . . in an art foreign to me but which I appreciate."

Early Problems. An early attempt to film *The Good Earth* on location in China failed miserably, primarily due to interference from the Chinese government, which was anxious to see a favorable impression of its new social order conveyed to the rest of the world. According to Buck's publisher and second husband, Richard Walsh,

Ch'i Pai-Shih's *The Return Home* (The National Gallery, Prague, Czech Republic), a 1931 ink-and-paint scroll, evokes the Chinese countryside that serves as the bold backdrop to Buck's *The Good Earth*. Buck stresses in her fiction that the land is to be experienced and not possessed.

Actress Luise Rainer played the role of O-Lan in Metro-Goldwyn-Mayer's 1937 film production of Buck's best-known work, *The Good Earth*.

Chinese bureaucrats, worried that the farmers would appear old-fashioned, insisted that they plow with modern tractors instead of the traditional water buffalo. Bureaucrats argued that the entire cast should be attired in new clothes and that buildings be freshly painted. Attempts were also made to have the younger actresses wear flowers over their ears. The Chinese bureaucrats finally acquiesced in the shooting of realistic backgrounds, but when these arrived in Hollywood, they had been ruined by acid poured into the cans, rumored to be deliberate sabotage.

The Final Product. The cost of the film ran to almost three million dollars, a large amount at the time, but it made a handsome profit of a half-million dollars, as well as a considerable amount of prestige, for the producer, Metro-Goldwyn-Mayer. Much of the huge cost came from the creation of scenery to resemble that of northern China and the portrayal of traditional Chinese farming techniques.

The final product was advertised as "the glorious screen reproduction of the most vital novel of our times" and its faithfulness to the novel was hailed as "line by line . . . page by page . . . chapter by chapter." This is Hollywood exaggeration. The film was considerably shortened, many episodes were omitted, others were added, and the attributes of the characters were altered. Most drastic changes occurred in the action. In the novel, the combined efforts of Wang and O-Lan enable them to purchase more land until a famine drives them south to Nanking, where they witness scenes of revolution and acquire money and jewelry that enable them to return home and purchase even more land. Wang buys a concubine, Lotus; O-Lan dies; and Wang disowns his eldest son for his improper attentions to Lotus. Wang's land is then inundated by a flood, and his house is temporarily occupied by revolutionists. In his old age he acquires another concubine, Peach Blossom.

In this photograph from 1902, a man looks out over the rice paddies and tea shrubs that punctuate the hills of Jiangxi in southeastern China.

In the film everything taking place after Wang and O-Lan's return from Nanking is dropped or softened. Lotus is an entertainer instead of a prostitute. Her liaison with the elder son that is unequivocally sexual in the novel is ambiguous in the film. She, therefore, becomes an insignificant foil to O-Lan, while the young concubine Peach Blossom is not even introduced. O-Lan, moreover, is transformed into a woman of beauty as well as strength. On her wedding day she plants a peach pit, a symbol of the land and its fertility. Wang in turn tells her that the land now "belongs to us both," a declaration completely incompatible with the widespread Confucian patriarchal system that Buck observed in the novel.

The film ends with O-Lan's death rather than Wang's. In the novel, as Wang breathes his last, he begs his sons for assurance that they will remain faithful to the land, which they give in a perfunctory manner indicating their opposite intentions. The film, however, ends as an elderly Wang utters the sentimental line, "O-Lan you are the earth," a neat reaffirmation of the theme of the land. In the novel neither Wang nor O-Lan is a conventional hero or heroine.

Rainer is pictured with actor Paul Muni (right), who played the role of Wang in the motion-picture adaptation of the Pulitzer Prize–winning book.

Wang's chief characteristics are tenacity and love of the land, neither of which is an outstanding virtue. O-Lan is a faithful wife but is otherwise illiterate and physically undistinguished. Both are embellished in the film to resemble a conventional Hollywood couple.

Presence of the Land. The film's pictorial achievements are outstanding in presenting the physical aspects of the land, both through panoramic shots and closeups of farmers driving their oxen through the soil. The film excels also in a fifteen-minute-long portrayal of a plague of locusts, a masterpiece of cinematography that it is only a brief interlude in the novel. In the novel, moreover, the locusts are less a symbol of nature's power than a test of the characters' ability to adapt. In the film, however, the plague assumes gigantic, almost supernatural, proportions. As the locusts are eventually driven off, they help bring about a reconciliation between Wang and his eldest son.

SOURCES FOR FURTHER STUDY

Chauhan, Pradyumna S. "Pearl Buck's *The Good Earth*: The Novel as Epic." In *The Several Worlds of Pearl S. Buck: Essays Presented at a Centennial Symposium, Randolph-Macon Woman's College, March 26–28, 1992*, edited by Elizabeth J. Lipscomb, Frances E. Webb, and Peter Conn. Westport, Conn.: Greenwood Press, 1994.

Conn, Peter. *Pearl S. Buck: A Cultural Biography*. New York: Cambridge University Press, 1996.

Hoban, James L., Jr. "Scripting The Good Earth; Versions of the Novel for the Screen." In *The Several Worlds of Pearl S. Buck: Essays Presented at a Centennial Symposium, Randolph-Macon Woman's College, March 26–28, 1992*, edited by Elizabeth J. Lipscomb, Frances E. Webb, and Peter Conn. Westport, Conn.: Greenwood Press, 1994.

THE GOOD EARTH

Genre: Novel
Subgenre: Family drama
Published: New York, 1931
Time period: Late nineteenth century
Setting: Northern China

Themes and Issues. Throughout her career, Pearl S. Buck compared and contrasted the cultures of China and the United States. This is true in *The Good Earth*, her masterpiece that sympathetically explores the problems of the Chinese farmer and, by extension, farmers of the American West. At the same time, Buck exposes the plight of Chinese women in a society that uniformly treats them as inferior to men. Buck subtly introduces the presence of Christianity but in such a way that the protagonist Wang does not understand its significance. She explores these topics indirectly as part of the cycle of birth and death in the fields, the farmer's hut, and the city. In so doing, she underscores the importance of willpower in the development of cultural patterns and individual behavior. Although *The Good Earth* has been classified as a "peasant epic," it depicts the human affinity with the earth that exists in all classes of society.

The Plot. Although the protagonist, Wang Lung, is born into poverty, he is not a pauper; he lives on a farm that has been in his family for many generations. When the time comes for him to take a wife, Wang follows his father's orders and buys a slave from the House of Hwang, the district's wealthiest family. This woman, O-Lan, is not beautiful, although perhaps a virgin, but she possesses the virtues most prized in a Chinese wife: good health, absolute obedience, and indefatigable industry.

O-Lan initially assumes only the duties of the household. Eventually she begins working in the fields at her husband's side, except for the brief periods during which her children are

In 1949 Buck established Welcome House Social Services, which selected and prepared parents for adopting orphaned, abandoned, and special-needs children from around the world. Buck is pictured above with a Welcome House child in the late 1960s.

born. Her first two children are boys, a welcome gift in Chinese society at that time. Males were given complete responsibility for carrying on the religious traditions and the everyday duties of the household. Girls were considered at best a burden, not really belonging to their parents but reared for marriage to other families. O-Lan's third child is a girl who is born mentally disabled.

Except for this misfortune, things go well at first for Wang. Through hard work and meticulous thrift, he is able to purchase additional land. However, disaster strikes in the form of a famine. Wang considers selling a portion of his land, but O-Lan intervenes, telling him to sell their household furnishings instead. He has no recourse but to go south to the city of Nanking, where he pulls a rickshaw, and O-Lan and the children beg in the streets. During a conflict between revolutionists and army forces, Wang and O-Lan join a horde of looters converging on an ornate residence. One of the inhabitants, taking Wang for a looter, gives him a sum of money. O-Lan discovers a hidden cache of jewelry.

Wang and O-Lan are now able to return to the farm, where O-Lan gives birth to twins, a boy and a girl. Wang is ashamed that he cannot read or write and sends his sons to school. The teacher gives them the names Nang Er and Nang Wan, the first word of each signifying "one whose wealth comes from the earth." During a period of massive flooding, Wang begins to visit prostitutes, becoming infatuated with one of them, Lotus, whom he eventually purchases. When the waters recede, he is happy to return to the land, and Lotus becomes only a toy or symbol. O-Lan, however, becomes mortally ill. Wang, finally realizing O-Lan's many sacrifices and his own neglect, weeps bitterly when she dies.

During this time Wang has been acquiring more and more land, most of which he rents out. He goes to live in the town dwelling formerly occupied by the Hwangs and purchases a child slave, Peach Blossom, who eventually becomes his concubine. At the end of the novel, Wang moves back to his old farmhouse. On his death bed he makes his sons promise never to sell the land, but it is clear that they will not heed his wishes.

Analysis. The publishers of *The Good Earth* observed that it is "worthy of a place on the short shelf of mighty novels of the land." It traces "the whole cycle of life, its terrors, its passions, its persistent ambitions, and its meager rewards." Although it can also be read as a document of the world economic Depression of the 1930s, the novel's greatest influence has been in introducing the traditions of the Far East to Western readers. Its characters and situations, however, transcending any single locality or culture, are universal in scope.

SOURCES FOR FURTHER STUDY

Chauhan, Pradyumna S. "Pearl S. Buck's *The Good Earth*: The Novel as Epic." In *The Several Worlds of Pearl S. Buck: Essays Presented at a Centennial Symposium, Randolph-Macon Woman's College, March 26–28, 1992*, edited by Elizabeth J. Lipscomb, Frances E. Webb, and Peter Conn. Westport, Conn.: Greenwood Press, 1992.

Hayford, Charles W. "*The Good Earth*, Revolution, and the American Raj in China." In *The Several Worlds of Pearl S. Buck: Essays Presented at a Centennial Symposium, Randolph-Macon Woman's College, March 26–28, 1992*, edited by Elizabeth J. Lipscomb, Frances E. Webb, and Peter Conn. Westport, Conn.: Greenwood Press, 1992.

Yu, Yuh-Chao. *Pearl S. Buck's Fiction: A Cross-Cultural Interpretation*. Taipei, China: Academica Sinica, 1981.

IMPERIAL WOMAN

> **Genre:** Novel
> **Subgenre:** Historical fiction
> **Published:** New York, 1956
> **Time period:** 1850–1900
> **Setting:** Beijing, China

Themes and Issues. The imperial woman of the title is a renowned historical personage, Zi-Xi, the Empress Dowager of China, about whom six other novels had been written in the West before Buck's. It is universally accepted that the empress gained and maintained politi-

This photograph of the famed and fabled Empress Dowager, the subject of Buck's 1956 historical novel, *Imperial Woman*, was taken around 1900.

cal power through a combination of luck and determination and that she ruled firmly, autocratically, and, some say, cruelly. However, there is no agreement concerning her fundamental character or the methods by which she rose to supreme power. Some writers portray her as a femme fatale and others as the eternal feminine. Buck had to decide on this matter as well as many others, such as to what degree the system of eunuchs and concubines led to moral degeneration, and to what degree American missionaries were responsible for the Boxer Rebellion of 1900, in which Chinese forces attacked Europeans and Chinese Christians, with the intention of ousting foreigners from China.

The Plot. The teenage daughter of an obscure Manchu nobleman, Zi-Xi is chosen to enter the Imperial Palace as one of many concubines. At first failing to arouse the emperor's interest, she eventually provides him with an heir. After the emperor's death, this infant son succeeds to the throne, and his mother becomes coregent, a position she holds for eleven years. Once the emperor comes of age, he reigns for only three years before his death. Zi-Xi again becomes coregent to the new emperor, this time for thirteen years. When this new emperor comes of age and takes the throne, he is unable to cope with Zi-Xi's maneuvering at court and eventually rules in name only under her management for the following ten years, after which they die within a few hours of each other.

This much is fact, but there are major questions about which historians and other novelists disagree and to which Buck was forced to respond. Had the man whom Zi-Xi appointed to head the Palace Guard been her sweetheart before she became a palace concubine? Had she lost her virginity before entering the palace? Was the emperor or another person the father of her child? Did she murder the next emperor, her own son, because he was showing signs of spirited independence? Did she have a succession of lovers throughout her reign? With one exception Buck answered these intriguing questions in the negative. The exception concerns the empress's relationship with the imperial guardsman. Buck recognizes that the two were close to each other as children but denies any sexual contact until Zi-Xi entered the palace.

Analysis. Buck had some difficulty reconciling the contradictory aspects of Zi-Xi's personality. Buck's preface indicates that the Empress Dowager "was a woman so devious in her gifts, so contradictory in her behavior, so rich in the many aspects of her personality, that it is difficult to comprehend and convey her whole self." Buck attributes some of Zi-Xi's ruthlessness to the crucial period of history during which China was trying to resist the encroachment of Western nations. She affirms, moreover, that in her analysis of Zi-Xi's character, which is generally more charitable than that of other novelists, she relied to a great degree on information she had absorbed during her residence in China. She may also have been aware of resemblances between her own motivations and reactions and those attributed to the Empress Dowager. These common threads, however, did not prevent Buck from following the historical record in a brilliant compromise with her own imagination.

SOURCES FOR FURTHER STUDY

Chung, Sue Fawn. "The Much Maligned Empress Dowager: A Revisionist Study of the Empress Dowager Tz'u-hsi (1838–1908)." In *Modern Asian Studies* 13, no. 2 (1979).

Liao, Kang. *Pearl S. Buck: A Cultural Bridge Across the Pacific.* Westport, Conn.: Greenwood Press, 1997.

Stirling, Nora B. *Pearl S. Buck: A Woman in Conflict.* Piscataway, N.J.: New Century Publishers, 1983.

THE TOWNSMAN

   Genre: Novel
   Subgenre: Rural domestic drama
   Published: New York, 1945
   Time period: 1860–1910
   Setting: Kansas

Themes and Issues. For many years Buck had been known mainly as a female author of

Chinese women with bound feet sit with their sons in southern China or Taiwan around 1900. In her fiction, Buck asserts that male-dominated societies, whether of the East or the West, present women with equal challenges. Buck chose a masculine pseudonym when she wrote her novel *The Townsmen* because she felt that men have fewer handicaps than women.

books about China. She sought a new identity as an American writer and decided to write about the origin and development of a Kansas town. To mask her identity, she chose a pseudonym, John Sedges. She chose this masculine name, she later explained, "because men have fewer 'handicaps in our society' than women have." Buck's protagonist is also masculine—not a typical Western cattle-herder or farmer, but rather a schoolteacher and founder of an urban society. He is "a modest fellow who refuses to ride wild horses, be a cowboy, shoot pistols into the air, kill his enemies, find gold in any hills, destroy Indians, or even get drunk."

Although Buck does not venture into the pallid atmosphere of local color writing, she retains *The Good Earth*'s theme of the land, not as something to be possessed, but as something, like water and sky, to be experienced. The protagonist also resembles Wang of *The Good Earth*, rising from near indigence to an established position in society. Buck herself, moreover, has much in common with her protagonist, an English expatriate; she and her hero both experience a culture radically different from that in which they were reared. Although the protagonist and the presumed author of the novel are both masculine, the concept of gender equality underlines nearly every chapter.

The Plot. A father leaves his English seacoast village to seek adventure in the American West with his wife, sons, and daughters. They travel from New York to Kansas by train and continue by horse-drawn cart to their final destination, Median, a cluster of a half-dozen sod dwellings. After building their own sod hut, the father insists on going farther west with his wife, but his son Jonathan, the protagonist, refuses to leave, working in the local store and teaching the neighbors' children at home.

Jonathan's dwelling is built with the aid of a former slave, whose son, Beaumont, becomes one of his pupils. Jonathan discovers that Beaumont is extremely intelligent, and that Beaumont's real father had been a wealthy aristocrat in New Orleans. Jonathan thereupon writes a letter to Beaumont's grandfather and receives a curt reply asking for proof of his birth. When Jonathan personally goes to New Orleans to present Beaumont's case, he meets Evan, a lawyer who arranges for Beaumont to be sent to Paris to train to become a brain surgeon.

Evan decides to return with Jonathan to Median and set up a practice there. After a short time Evan tries to turn Median into a cattle town to attract money from out of state, but Jonathan insists on maintaining the small town's family-oriented atmosphere. After the issue is put to a vote, which Evan loses, he moves to Topeka.

Jonathan falls in love with Judy, the daughter of an itinerant evangelist, and proposes marriage. Jonathan's mother then reappears, during another of many pregnancies caused by her husband's frequent sexual demands. She immediately gives birth and dies an hour later. Her funeral is held on the day originally scheduled for Jonathan's wedding. When Judy is setting out for the funeral, Evan arrives; they suddenly kiss and resolve to leave Median, marry, and start a new life together in Topeka.

Jonathan eventually marries a local girl, Katie, neither lively nor pretty, but faithful and hardworking. He gives up teaching and takes over his father-in-law's store. Katie has a fatal stroke, for which Jonathan feels guilt even though he is not responsible. Evan's sister, Laura, who realizes Jonathan still loves Judy, makes a special trip to inform him that Evan has taken his secretary as his mistress and that

Judy is very unhappy. A year later, Judy's father, now insane, shoots and kills Evan. Jonathan visits Judy, hoping that she will return his feelings, but he soon realizes that she never will love him. Jonathan sails for England, where his former pupil Beaumont meets him. Beaumont is now a famed brain surgeon, prosperous and blissfully married. After a cursory visit to his birthplace, Jonathan returns to Median, where he is welcomed at the station by the townspeople and taken to the site of a high school under construction, which is to be named in his honor.

Analysis. *The Townsman* addresses both the weak and the strong points of American life. Jonathan's mother suffers from the domination of his father, and Beaumont's family silently endures racial discrimination. The book was written during World War II, and Beaumont predicts that if the American heart does not grow "to comprehend the brotherhood of man, she'll be torn in two when the big war comes." One of the early settlers of Median affirms that he does not believe in "educatin' colored people, Indians and females." Jonathan himself recognizes that one of the shortcomings of democracy is that "common folk were common folk." Still, all of the townspeople join in erecting a high school in his honor. The book is in part a tribute to the teaching profession. Jonathan stands as an example of the ideal male, who masters the elements and treats his family and neighbors with truth, fidelity, and kindness.

SOURCES FOR FURTHER STUDY

Block, Irvin. *The Lives of Pearl Buck: A Tale of China and America.* New York: Crowell, 1973.

Conn, Peter. "Pearl S. Buck and American Literary Culture." In *The Several Worlds of Pearl S. Buck: Essays Presented at a Centennial Symposium, Randolph-Macon Woman's College, March 26–28, 1992,* edited by Elizabeth J. Lipscomb, Frances E. Webb, and Peter Conn. Westport, Conn.: Greenwood Press, 1992.

Stirling, Nora B. *Pearl S. Buck: A Woman in Conflict.* Piscataway, N.J.: New Century Publishers, 1983.

Other Works

THE PATRIOT (1939). This novel deals with the internal struggles in China between radicals and the government just prior to the war with Japan in the late 1930s. I-wan, the son of a wealthy banker, is mistakenly sent to jail. There he meets En-lan, a young revolutionist peasant. I-wan insists when the jailer comes to release him that En-lan also be set free. Eventually the two become blood brothers, and I-wan accepts En-lan's radical ideas.

To keep I-wan from the army, however, his father sends him to Japan to live with a business associate, Muraki. I-wan enters Muraki's employ and becomes attracted to his daughter, Tama, who wavers between modern ideas and conservative traditions of female submissiveness. Muraki wants Tama to marry an older, widowed general. With the nation on the brink of war, she believes she must marry in patriotic duty. When the threat of war recedes, however, I-wan asks for Tama's hand and sends a matchmaker to the family. Muraki replies in the negative, but Tama cuts her wrists, forcing her father to relent.

After hostilities eventually break out between China and Japan, I-wan and Tama feel torn between their national loyalties and their mutual love. Tama moves into separate sleeping quarters, and I-wan decides that he must return to China, not because of animosity toward Japan, but to imitate the inherent patriotism of the Japanese. He believes that, whether his country is right or wrong, his duty is to remain loyal and returns to take a place in the army.

The subject of Thomas Eakins's 1899 oil painting *The Dean's Roll Call* (Museum of Fine Arts, Boston) reflects Brother André's role as mentor and guide to Mrs. Wu in Buck's novel *Pavilion of Women*. The harmonious balance struck between Brother André and Mrs. Wu indicates that Buck's themes are universal.

PAVILION OF WOMEN (1946). Forty-year-old Mrs. Wu tells one of her sons that she is going to invite her husband to take a concubine. The son objects, noting that the age difference between Mr. Wu and a young girl might lead to the concubine's children being the same age or younger than his grandchildren. Mrs. Wu dismisses her son's argument and employs a matchmaker who finds Ch'iuming, an orphan who had been abandoned in the city and raised on a farm. Ch'iuming is healthy and able to work but cannot read.

After Mrs. Wu engages a Western priest, Brother André, to teach English to another of her sons, she becomes curious about the priest's philosophy. She learns that his religion is unorthodox and based on nature, which strikes a sympathetic chord in her. When another of her sons has trouble adjusting to his wife's modern views, Mrs. Wu contrives to send him to study in the West. When Ch'iuming becomes pregnant, Mr. Wu visits prostitutes. Ch'iuming tries to hang herself, but Brother André saves her with an injection, enabling her to bear her child, who is consigned to Brother André's care. He tells Mrs. Wu that she is guilty of three sins: harming her husband, harming Ch'iuming, and being proud. She offers to return to Mr. Wu, but he is now happy with a prostitute much more to his liking than Ch'iuming, who remains in the family but has nothing more to do with him.

Brother André is mortally wounded by thieves, but before his death he asks Mrs. Wu to care for twenty abandoned teenage girls. She agrees, realizing at the same time that she loves him. With Brother André in mind, she arranges a productive future for her household. Her son returns from the United States and sets up a country school. Ch'iuming and one of her daughters-in-law go to live in the same village. Mrs. Wu, under the influence of Brother André's philosophy and conscious of her own mortality, realizes that she had been trying unsuccessfully to organize her life by material means and has found contentment only in the spiritual.

THIS PROUD HEART (1938). In her collection of essays *Of Men and Women*, Pearl S. Buck observed both the general discontentment of American women and their marked lack of enjoyment of men. In arguing for gender equality, she also affirmed that while men had the good jobs, women were designated for the "engine room" of society. *This Proud Heart* had previously presented in fictional form these and other notions concerning gender equality. June, a young girl with enormous talent in sculpture, is engaged to a shy, unpretentious young man. She takes more pleasure in making and serving her wedding cake than in eating it, a symbol of her dedication to art and activity. She adorns everything she touches and has so much success in selling her sculptures that she realizes that she could earn much more money than her husband.

After June gives birth to her first child, an eminent artist offers to give her lessons. Although her desire to create becomes stronger than her desire for home, husband, or children, she tells her husband that she wants another child so that she may feel an equality between them. After the birth of her second child, she is contented but suspects that she would feel even happier if she were able to be more creative.

At about the same time that one of June's statues wins a prize, her husband dies. She then goes to Paris for further study, where she meets another American artist, whom she marries. When she decides she must resume her own artistic activities, he does not oppose her but insists that she work in clay rather than in the more difficult marble, on the grounds that only two or three great sculptors dare to use marble. In the words of the title, her proud heart makes her ask indignantly how he knows she is not one of the great. She rents a studio and learns that one of her former models, a Russian dancer, has become her husband's mistress. June confronts him with her knowledge of the liaison but does not leave him.

The artist who had originally given June lessons now offers to sponsor her in a coming show. Her proud heart, however, keeps her

The still life *Chinese Patron of the Arts* (The Bowers Museum of Culture, Santa Ana, California) by Evylena Nunn Miller evokes the balance and order the artist seeks. In *This Proud Heart,* the sacrifices June makes in order to become a successful sculptor mirrors the challenges of Buck's own life as a writer and woman.

from accepting. When her husband openly reveals his jealousy of her success and refuses to attend her father's funeral, she decides that she no longer needs him. Despite everything, she must consider whether he needs her. At their final interview, polite and without passion, she realizes the relationship is over, and he leaves. She does not know whether she will grieve for him, but she knows that work will take his place.

THE THREE DAUGHTERS OF MADAME LIANG (1969). Despite its title, this novel is more about Mrs. Liang and her political environment than about her daughters. Fifty-four

years old and separated from her husband, Mrs. Liang is the owner of the most fashionable restaurant in communist China. Her three daughters live in the United States. Grace, the eldest, a research botanist, is ordered by the communist regime to return to Shanghai to carry on her research. The second daughter, Mercy, a musician, marries John Sung, a nuclear physicist who wants to return to China. Because the two cannot obtain clearance, they go first to England and from there to China. They are warmly received until John refuses to work on germ-warfare projects to be used against the United States and is condemned to hard labor on the land. Joy, the youngest daughter, an artist, falls in love with a famous Chinese painter in New York who is bitterly anticommunist. As a result she never returns to her native land.

Through Mrs. Liang's intervention, John is finally released and sent to a nuclear research unit but is killed during the tryout of a nuclear warhead. Mercy, now thoroughly disenchanted with the regime, persuades one of her music pupils to pretend to be her brother and escort her to the southern border. She crosses safely, but her student is arrested. Grace falls in love with a communist official and continues to support the system. Mrs. Liang is beaten to death by a gang of young revolutionists in front of her restaurant. Grace, the only daughter at the funeral, resolves to stay in China. Mrs. Liang before her death had realized that the communists, by banishing traditional religion, had created a vacuum filled by worship of the system and its chairman. Without a spiritual basis such as that of the ancient philosophers, the nation would be continually attempting to balance social order and freedom.

Resources

Collections of Pearl S. Buck's manuscripts and letters may be found in libraries of the following institutions: University of Alabama, Columbia University, University of Florida, Haverford College, University of Iowa, University of Michigan, University of Mississippi, New York Public Library, New York University, University of Oregon, Pennsylvania State University, Randolph-Macon Woman's College, Radcliffe College, Smith College, Syracuse University, Tulane University, University of Vermont, University of Virginia, State Historical Society of Wisconsin, and Yale University. Other sources of interest to students of Pearl S. Buck include the following:

Pearl S. Buck International (PSBI). The many humanitarian assistance organizations founded by Buck during her lifetime have merged as Pearl S. Buck International. PSBI is dedicated to improving the lives and opportunities of children worldwide, with particular emphasis on programs in Asia. (http://www.pearl-s-buck.org/psbi)

Pearl S. Buck House. The former home of Pearl S. Buck in Perkasie, Pennsylvania, was made a National Historic Landmark in 1980. Buck lived in the ten-room 1835 stone farmhouse for thirty-eight years. The tour includes a blend of American and Asian antiques and art, as well as a display of Buck's many literary and humanitarian awards, including the Nobel and Pulitzer Prizes in Literature. (http://www.pearl-s-buck.org/psbi.PSBHouse/visiting.asp)

Pearl S. Buck Birthplace. Buck's ancestral home in Hillsboro, West Virginia, is now a museum devoted to her life and work that is open daily for guided tours from May to November and by appointment.

Audiotape. Buck's novel *Letter from Peking* (1957) is available on audiocassette.

A. OWEN ALDRIDGE

Truman Capote

BORN: September 30, 1924, New Orleans, Louisiana
DIED: August 25, 1984, Bel-Air, California
IDENTIFICATION: Mid- to late-twentieth-century fiction and prose writer known as much for his jet-setting reputation as for his southern gothic short stories and reportorial fiction.

Truman Capote established himself early as a precocious literary wunderkind. He began writing at a time when fiction and reportage were widely different modes of writing. His early works, which focused on southern locales and people, drew critical praise for their vivid atmospheres and characterizations. His most famous book, *In Cold Blood* (1966), a critical and popular success, showed that a writer could make great literature out of real events. This innovative approach to fiction, which he called a "nonfiction novel," generated much publicity. Although Capote's later work never attained the success of this novel, he established himself as a leader in the new fiction, and other novelists were quick to follow his lead.

The Writer's Life

Truman Capote was born Truman Streckfus Persons on September 30, 1924, in New Orleans, Louisiana. His parents, Lillie Mae Faulk and Arch Persons, had recently moved from Alabama. Arch tried many jobs and was often on the edge of the law with his many schemes and shady dealings. His parents' marriage dissolved after seven years, and in 1930 Capote was left with Lillie Mae's relations in Monroeville, Alabama. His new household consisted of three middle-aged Faulk sisters and their older brother.

Considered effeminate and soft, as a child Capote was often ostracized by the other boys in his town. His unconventional spirit, however, would lead him to create a new literary genre, the nonfiction novel. He is pictured here surrounded by dolls and toys in 1948, shortly after the publication of *Other Voices, Other Rooms*.

Childhood. Although he was considered a "sissy," Capote was a bright and likable child. He befriended his young neighbor Harper Lee, who would later write *To Kill a Mockingbird* (1960) and model one of its characters, Dill, on Capote. Meanwhile, Lillie Mae had traveled to New York City and married Joseph Garcia Capote, a successful businessman. In 1932 she brought her son to join them in New York. Adopted by Joe in 1935, the boy took the name Truman Garcia Capote. In Brooklyn, Capote lived a comfortable life, vacationing in Cuba, in Bermuda, and twice in Europe and frequently visiting Monroeville.

In high school, Capote decided to become a writer and to rebel against convention. He began failing classes and refused to take physical education. He landed a job at *The New Yorker* but was fired after angering the poet Robert Frost. He turned to writing full-time, moving briefly to New Orleans to work on *Other Voices, Other Rooms* (1948) and then back to New York, where he published some short stories in *Harper's Bazaar* and *Mademoiselle* in 1945. In 1947 he was among a group of young writers featured in *Life* magazine and was by then considered a promising writer, although he had published only short stories.

Growing Stature. When *Other Voices, Other Rooms* finally appeared in 1948, it became a bestseller and caused a great stir, partly because of the dust jacket photograph of Capote lying on a sofa, staring seductively at the camera. This experience taught Capote that his private life could generate as much publicity as his writing, and perhaps more. He moved into his own apartment, away from his mother, with whom he had a problematic relationship. When *A Tree of Night and Other Stories* was published in 1949, Capote left again for Europe, this time with a new companion, Jack Dunphy, with whom he would have a longtime relationship. The two traveled to Ischia, an island off the coast of Italy where Capote could write, then to the Moroccan port of Tangier, and then back to New York. Out of these travels came, in 1950, his third book, *Local Color*, which received favorable reviews.

Full Maturity. In 1952 Capote published *The Grass Harp: A Play*, which was produced on stage that year. He worked feverishly on the adaptation, and when the play closed after only twenty-six performances, he relieved his disappointment by traveling to Taormina, an Italian commune northeast of Sicily. While he was in Europe in 1953, director John Huston hired him to write the screenplay for *Beat the Devil* (1954). Shortly into the new year, Capote's mother died, and, soon after, his stepfather was imprisoned for embezzlement. After his release, Joe turned to his stepson for financial help, which Capote provided. Capote's next play, *House of Flowers*, written with Harold Arlen, was published in 1954 and produced in 1955 and ran for five months. He continued to make new friends in society, including Marilyn Monroe, Elizabeth Taylor, and Jacqueline Kennedy.

At the end of 1955, Capote, now interested in journalism, traveled to the Soviet Union with the touring company of *Porgy and Bess*. The result was *The Muses Are Heard* (1956),

An infectious gadabout or a social climber? Capote had a knack for ingratiating himself to some of the leading luminaries of the day. Here he dances with actress Marilyn Monroe at the El Morocco in New York in 1955.

which showcased Capote's talent for reporting conversations and describing scenes. The success of *The Muses Are Heard* whetted his appetite for journalism, so he went to the Far East and interviewed the film star Marlon Brando. Returning from Greece in 1958, Capote found *Breakfast at Tiffany's: A Short Novel and Three Stories* already in the book-

Contributing to the dazzle of Capote's now-legendary masked party at the Plaza Hotel on November 28, 1966 were such socialites and celebrities as Mrs. Nicholas Katzenbach (upper left), Mrs. Henry Ford (upper right), actress Joan Fontaine (lower left), and Princess Lee Radziwell (lower right).

Masked revelers at Capote's infamous 1966 masked party included singer Frank Sinatra and his wife, actress Mia Farrow.

stores, prompting several female friends to claim they were the model for the book's protagonist, Holly Golightly.

In November, 1959, *The New York Times* reported the murder of a wealthy farmer, Herb Clutter, and his family in Holcomb, Kansas. Sensing the case's literary potential, Capote and Harper Lee went to Kansas to gather material for a book. He left for Europe to write it but interrupted his work to write the screenplay for *The Innocents* (1961). Delays in the executions of the killers postponed the finish of *In Cold Blood* until 1965. When parts of the novel finally appeared in *The New Yorker* in 1966, it was immediately recognized as a masterpiece. It made Capote even more famous and earned him enough money to ease his financial woes. He celebrated by throwing a masked ball at the Plaza Hotel, to which he invited the rich and famous, as well as friends he had made during his time in Kansas. The press called it the party of the century.

Decline. Following his greatest success, Capote began a downward slide in his private and professional life. Increasingly dependent on prescription pills and alcohol, he kept postponing his work on *Answered Prayers: The Unfinished Novel* (1986). In 1967 he retreated to Palm Springs, California, to write, but he also continued his television appearances and travels to Europe. By then, Jack Dunphy had left him, and Capote began a series of relationships with young men. By 1974 he was no further along on *Answered Prayers*, but *Esquire* magazine finally published part of the unfinished novel. Capote's society friends were outraged to discover their conversations with him reproduced in print. Most of them ended their relationships with him. Though outwardly unrepentant, he never got over the rejection, and his feelings of betrayal and isolation only increased his self-destructive behavior.

Capote's role in the 1976 film *Murder by Death* became for him a public embarrassment.

HIGHLIGHTS IN CAPOTE'S LIFE

1924   Truman Capote is born Truman Streckfus Persons on September 30 in New Orleans, Louisiana.

1932   Moves to New York to live with his mother and her new husband, Joseph Garcia Capote.

1935   Adopted by stepfather and takes the name Truman Garcia Capote.

1935–1943 Attends private schools in New York; decides to become a writer.

1945   Publishes short stories in *Harper's Bazaar* and *Mademoiselle*.

1947   Featured in *Life* magazine.

1948   Publishes *Other Voices, Other Rooms*; tours Europe.

1949   Publishes *A Tree of Night and Other Stories*; returns to Europe.

1950   Publishes *Local Color*.

1952   Publishes *The Grass Harp: A Play*, which is produced unsuccessfully.

1953   Writes screenplay for *Beat the Devil*.

1955   *House of Flowers* is produced on Broadway; Capote travels to Soviet Union with the cast of *Porgy and Bess*; works on *The Muses Are Heard*.

1959   Capote goes to Kansas to gather material for a book on the Clutter murders.

1961   Writes screenplay for *The Innocents*.

1966   Publishes *In Cold Blood* to immediate success.

1967–1979 Experiences slow decline resulting from irregular work habits, disruptive personal relationships, and rejection by former friends.

1979–1980 Briefly buoyed by success of "Handcarved Coffins" and *Music for Chameleons*.

1981–1983 Suffers continually worsening health.

1984   Dies on August 25 in Bel-Air, California.

1986   *Answered Prayers: The Unfinished Novel* is published posthumously.

1987   *A Capote Reader* is published posthumously.

TRUMAN CAPOTE
MUSIC FOR CHAMELEONS

"Electrifying…a knockout. Capote's alacrity and cunning makes this his most enjoyable book."—*Newsweek*

A brief spurt of creativity in 1979 produced his last major work, "Handcarved Coffins," and he was buoyed by the success of *Music for Chameleons* in 1980. Soon, however, he was suffering hallucinations resulting from drug and alcohol abuse. Throughout the early 1980s, he was frequently hospitalized as his health continually worsened. Finally, in August of 1984, he flew to California to stay with Joanne Carson, one of the few friends who had remained loyal to him. On August 25, she found him dead in one of her bedrooms.

The Writer's Work

From the beginning of his writing career, Truman Capote captured his readers' imaginations with his entrancing subtlety of style and precise use of language. His early fiction has a dreamlike quality and great evocative power; his later fiction and nonfiction alike display vivid imagery and graceful prose.

Issues in Capote's Writing. Despite the diversity of Capote's work, some fundamental issues link his stories. A principal concern in his writing is the individual as outsider, a person who is a part of but separate from social surroundings, be they a family or society at large. Often Capote focuses on characters who are different by virtue of their independent spirit, such as Holly Golightly, or alienated because they have been somehow maimed or victimized, such as Perry Smith. In some cases, a family's unity has been destroyed because of an eccentricity or defect in character, reflecting Capote's own upbringing. Especially in his early fiction, Capote centers his tales around children who are bewildered by their surroundings, entranced by other people, and in search of a place and identity.

Themes. Certain themes may be found in all of Capote's stories: universal loneliness, the binding power of love, loss of innocence that

Capote, in a quieter moment, relaxes on the sofa in his Brooklyn Heights apartment in New York in 1958.

either matures or distorts individual character, dangers lurking in the shadows, the individual's relation to others and to society, and the importance of independence and freedom. In Capote's world, one finds a resolute will to withhold judgment of those who are honest with themselves. Truth and trust are intertwined, and to be genuine is to win Capote's approval, however different from the social norm one may be.

Of himself, Capote said that he did not have vices, and of his characters, that the ordinary vices did not seem to matter. What does matter to him is honesty, sincerity, reliability. He condemned those who betrayed their friends' trust, and treachery of this sort was anathema to him. The villains in his novels are conniving, manipulative, untrustworthy people, such as Dr. Morris Ritz in *The Grass Harp*. One sus-

pects that Capote admired Perry Smith, the murderous ex-convict of *In Cold Blood*, because he is a soulful character true in purpose, speech, and action. By contrast, Capote disliked Dick Hickock, whose character is not much different from that of Dr. Ritz.

Capote's early stories are set in rural southern locales. His characters are singular, sharply drawn, and often mysterious and strange. Several early stories are concerned with a young man finding his place and himself in new surroundings among new people. When Capote arrived in New York City, he discovered other people and situations that shifted his focus to interesting, defiantly different characters. He had an attraction to the sordid, seedy elements of life, and the two killers he came to know and study while writing *In Cold Blood* captured his imagination. In a curious way,

Capote became known for his flamboyant public persona as much as his polished, insightful prose. Here he attends a tenth anniversary party for pop artist Andy Warhol's magazine, *Interview*, at the posh New York disco club Studio 54 on June 7, 1979.

SOME INSPIRATIONS BEHIND CAPOTE'S WORK

Truman Capote admired the fiction of the British writer W. Somerset Maugham, and early in life he read the work of the American expatriate writer Henry James, whom he considered a masterful storyteller. Critics point to influences of the Southern writers William Faulkner, Eudora Welty, and Carson McCullers, but any influence these authors had on Capote had faded by the 1950s, when he was beginning to think of himself as the American Marcel Proust. Like Proust, the French novelist whose *À la recherche du temps perdu* (1913–1927; *Remembrance of Things Past*, 1922–1931, 1981) chronicled his life among the wealthy bourgeois and nobility of Paris, Capote hoped to use his charm and personality to enter high society and find characters for his fiction.

Capote himself said his literary mentor was Gustave Flaubert, the author of *Madame Bovary* (1857; English translation, 1886), famous for his precise literary style and perfectionism. Like Flaubert, Capote wrote his fiction with a clear purpose toward a well-defined conclusion. He endorsed Flaubert's distrust of inspiration, relying instead on reasoned judgment, calculation, and cool purpose. The author's invisible presence in all of Capote's fiction reflects Flaubert's principle that the author must be present everywhere, visible nowhere. Capote was continually inspired by Flaubert's high literary standards, and his difficulty with *Answered Prayers* may have derived partly from his inability to rise to those standards.

Like Truman Capote, artist Andy Warhol often turned to the famous for both inspiration and friendship. In *Jackie* (synthetic polymer paint and silkscreen ink on canvas), painted in 1963, he makes a highly public figure, then-First Lady Jacqueline Kennedy, the subject of his portrait (left). Years before, Capote found himself deep inside the cult of fame and the subject of his own Warhol portrait painted around 1955 (right).

Capote's graceful prose and literary taste gave these subjects a quality that in life they lacked.

Literary Legacy. Although the blending of journalism and fiction was not new, Capote brought to this literary form several qualities that set his work apart from that of others. The most striking feature in his reportorial writing is his fidelity to fact. Capote took scrupulous care to reproduce what he had seen and heard as accurately as he could. By all accounts, he had a superb memory and an exceptionally keen eye. He believed that journalism told of events in a linear fashion, staying on the surface.

By using the techniques of fiction—characterization, evocative description, and a careful selection and artful use of detail—Capote could go beneath the surface to reveal or instill meaning in people and events and their interrelation. He was exceptionally skilled at combining speech and action to depict a scene. His gift for comedy also lends a special element to his best writing, evident in *The Muses Are Heard* and *Breakfast at Tiffany's*. His comic talent has a light, sunny quality and sometimes a sly, almost wicked, playfulness.

Capote demonstrated that when real events are given shape and structure and when dialogue is realistic, reportage can become literature. When he writes about places, as he does in *Local Color*, he invariably focuses on people and on how they speak and behave, giving life to his descriptions. Color for him consists of interesting and amusing people interacting in unusual locales. His eye for detail, his talent for creating vivid and dramatic scenes, and his unwavering control of the sound and rhythm of sentences all give his writing a lasting value.

LONG FICTION

1948   Other Voices, Other Rooms
1951   The Grass Harp
1956   A Christmas Memory (serial)
1966   In Cold Blood
1967   The Thanksgiving Visitor (serial)
1986   Answered Prayers: The Unfinished Novel

SHORT FICTION

1949   A Tree of Night and Other Stories
1958   Breakfast at Tiffany's: A Short Novel and Three Stories
1983   One Christmas
1986   I Remember Grandpa: A Story
1985   Three by Truman Capote

PLAYS

1952   The Grass Harp: A Play
1954   House of Flowers (with Harold Arlen)

SCREENPLAYS

1954   Beat the Devil (with John Huston)
1961   The Innocents

NONFICTION

1950   Local Color
1956   The Muses Are Heard
1959   Observations (with Richard Avedon)
1973   The Dogs Bark: Public People and Private Places
1983   One Christmas

MISCELLANEOUS

1963   Selected Writings
1969   Trilogy: An Experiment in Multimedia (with Eleanor Perry and Frank Perry)
1980   Music for Chameleons
1987   A Capote Reader

The nineteenth-century French novelist Gustave Flaubert, seen here in an 1856 oil portrait by artist Eugene Giraud, was a powerful influence on Capote. Like Capote, Flaubert explored the uncontrollable impulses that often seethed beneath the calm exterior of his characters.

BIBLIOGRAPHY

Brinnin, John Malcolm. *Truman Capote: A Memoir*. London: Sidgwick & Jackson, 1987.

Clarke, Gerald. *Capote: A Biography*. New York: Simon and Schuster, 1988.

Garson, Helen S. *Truman Capote*. New York: Frederick Ungar, 1980.

Gray, Richard. "Aftermath: Southern Literature Since World War II." In *The Literature of Memory: Modern Writers of the American South*. Baltimore: Johns Hopkins University Press, 1977.

Grobel, Lawrence. *Conversations with Capote*. New York: New American Library, 1988.

Inge, M. Thomas. *Truman Capote: Conversations*. Jackson: University of Mississippi Press, 1987.

Nance, William L. *The Worlds of Truman Capote*. New York: Stein and Day, 1970.

Ozick, Cynthia. "Truman Capote Reconsidered." In *Art and Ardor*. New York: E. P. Dutton, 1983.

Reed, Kenneth T. *Truman Capote*. Boston: Twayne Publishers, 1981.

Stanton, Robert J. *Truman Capote: A Primary and Secondary Bibliography*. Boston: G. K. Hall, 1980.

Mixing Fiction and Reality

Truman Capote was fascinated all his life by the way things looked and by how people talked and behaved. As a novelist, he wanted to mold people into his own sense of how they should look and be. Style was his ruling passion, in writing especially, but also in every other aspect of life. His experiences as a child taught him about fear and the darker aspects of life. The haunting, ghostly images and bizarre characters of his early fiction reflect Capote's childhood imagination. However, this shadowy world, with its decaying past and ghostly perimeters, faded from his later fiction and was replaced by the glittering world of fame and fashion that Capote came to embrace fully. His masterpiece, *In Cold Blood* (1966), allowed him to conjure up some of the shadows of his dark childhood world, but in the form of a novel he could leave behind.

Journalistic Character Studies.

The man who was closest to Capote for most of his adult life, Jack Dunphy, said that Capote was an avid reader of magazines. This is not surprising, considering his gift for reportage and his fascination with events and personalities. Capote appreciated the style and the surface of things, but he also sensed the deeper truths beyond appearances, and if his intellect could not grasp a person or a situation, his imagination could create

a possible likeness. He loved to create fictional characters, but, just as much, if not more, he loved to create characters based on real people he encountered in his life, using not so much his imagination as his extraordinary memory. His art is in his use of language to shape a scene, reproduce dialogue, and imbue the whole with grace and vividness.

In the 1961 film version of *Breakfast at* Tiffany's, actress Audrey Hepburn portrays Holly Golightly, a woman who often chooses to filter her world through the protective cover of sunglasses. When reality was harsh and overbearing, Holly would retreat into decadence and the comfort of illusions.

Stylistic Dualities. Critics have long noted that Capote's writing has two sides, a dark side and a light side. His light stories, such as *Breakfast at Tiffany's* (1958), have the antic spirit that he often displayed. His dark stories, such as *Other Voices, Other Rooms* (1948), feature characters who are eccentric, lost, misshapen, lonely, and outcast. Even as late as *In Cold Blood*, Capote found expression for this side of his artistic vision in Perry Smith, the embodiment of his idea of the outcast, maimed, lost soul. The irony is that actual events would provide him with such an ideal subject. Novelist Norman Mailer charged Capote with a "failure of imagination" for using real events and people, but it can be argued that it takes great imagination to paint Capote's portrait of Perry Smith.

This still from the 1967 motion picture *In Cold Blood* conveys the dark side evident in much of Capote's work. Capote strongly identified with the character Perry Smith, played by actor Robert Blake (above); both Capote and Perry considered themselves outsiders, trying to find their place in the world.

Art and Instinct. Capote's "nonfiction novel," *In Cold Blood*, is a masterpiece in its successful unification of the two principal elements of his work: the reporter's instinct and sharp eye for significant detail and the novelist's ability to turn detail into art. Significantly, some of Capote's best books are collections of writings that combine reportage and fiction. His early tales mine the quarry of his childhood, and when he had exhausted that source, he turned to his life in New York and Europe, focusing as he always had on the character of places and the essence of the people who caught his eye. His interest in high society—with its stylish women and powerful figures, its glittering ambience and unceasing activity, its dynamism and amorality—all compelled his attention and stimulated his artistic ambitions.

One of Capote's fundamental impulses was to repeat what he heard and to describe what he saw. Little of his writing focuses on himself. Only at the end does he turn the focus toward himself, and when he does, the novelist loses touch, even interest. As early as *The Grass Harp* (1951), his protagonist confesses that he may have betrayed someone's trust by repeating what the person said. Judge Cool says, "What one says hardly matters, only the trust with which it is said. . . ." Judge Cool's comment does not resolve the conflict between trust and telling, and events proved to Capote the novelist and reporter that the two do not always mix.

This dilemma would follow Capote to the end of his life. His decision to repeat the secrets of his friends in *Answered Prayers: The Unfinished Novel* (1986) destroyed his social life by betraying the trust his friends had placed in him. His greatest success, *In Cold Blood*, blended fact and fiction in an imaginative creation. His greatest failure occurred when he made his friends his fiction.

SOURCES FOR FURTHER STUDY

Mengeling, Marvin E. *The Critical Response to Truman Capote*. Westport, Conn.: Greenwood Press, 1999.

Plimpton, George. *Truman Capote: In Which Various Friends, Enemies, Acquaintances, and Detractors Recall His Turbulent Career*. New York: Anchor Books, 1998.

Waldmeir, Joseph J., and John Christian Waldmeir, eds. *The Critical Response to Truman Capote*. Westport, Conn.: Greenwood Press, 1999.

Reader's Guide to Major Works

THE GRASS HARP

Genre: Novel
Subgenre: Gothic romance
Published: New York, 1951
Time period: 1930s
Setting: Small town in rural Alabama

Themes and Issues. The central themes of Truman Capote's tale include love, companionship, truth, trust, togetherness, loyalty, loneliness, and self-discovery. When Dolly Talbo confesses her loneliness to him, Judge Cool proposes marriage. She later recalls that he told her "love is a chain of love" that binds people together.

After his aunt Dolly's death, Collin Fenwick feels that his life has been "a series of closed circles." His decision to go away and become a lawyer closes one circle, and he prepares to leap into the next. Love makes one complete, both within oneself and within one's circle of companions; it also brings understanding. After fearing that his friend Riley Henderson has betrayed him, Collin finally realizes that their friendship is too strong for such a betrayal. Love generates trust and frees people from having to hide who they are. In the character of Dr. Morris Ritz, the novel shows what becomes of a person who has no truth and cannot love.

The Plot. When his mother dies, Collin Fenwick is taken by his father to live with Collin's two aunts, Dolly and Verena Talbo, who have a "shadowy house on Talbo Lane" in a small southern town. Catherine Creek, a black woman, hired by the sisters' father as an

In *The Grass Harp* Capote explores some of the many forms of love and companionship. By retreating into the woods, Dolly Talbot and Judge Cool are able to leave behind the small-town isolation that has led to their sense of loneliness. The above still is from the 1995 movie, which starred actress Piper Laurie as Dolly and actor Walter Matthau as Judge Cool.

orphaned child, has become Dolly's best friend and lives in a little house in the backyard. A "loud and prying boy of eleven" when he arrives, Collin immediately takes to Dolly, the older sister, who is like a shadow in the corner. Gentle and spiritual, Dolly at first would flee at the sound of Collin's footsteps or fold "like the petals of shy-lady fern." She gathers herbs in River Wood and brews a secret cure for dropsy, which she sells through the mail.

Collin's favorite place is the house's spooky attic. Through cracks in the attic floor, he can watch Dolly at work in the kitchen. Verena, the dictator of the house and a formidable owner of several businesses in town, also has a dark side. Sometimes at night, alone in her room, she looks at snapshots of a young lady who betrayed her, then turns out the lights and paces the floor. Soon one hears "a hurt rusty crying sound as though she'd tripped and fallen in the dark." Verena goes to Chicago on business and returns with Dr. Morris Ritz, a shady gentleman who winks first one eye, then the other, wears "razzledazzle, dagger-sharp shoes," and carries an ominous-looking briefcase. Verena and Dr. Ritz plan to open a factory, but first they want to take over Dolly's mail-order business. When Dolly refuses to give them the formula, an argument ensues, and Dolly leaves, taking Catherine and Collin with her. They seek refuge in a tree house near River Wood.

Riley Henderson, out hunting, joins them. The sheriff arrives with a reverend, a deputy, and the retired Judge Cool. When he fails to persuade the runaways to come down from the tree, the sheriff retreats. Judge Cool, who is attracted to Dolly, remains, and the five of them spend the night together in the tree house. The next morning when Riley and Collin undress and go into the river together, Collin discovers that "there began in him an affectionate feeling for me that supported my own for him." This moment is followed by one of the book's most lyrical lines: "Leaves like scarlet hands floated on the green slow water." Dolly confesses her loneliness, and the judge proposes marriage.

Meanwhile, Dr. Ritz runs off with thousands of dollars he steals from Verena. Chastened by his treachery and her own poor judgment, Verena comes to ask Dolly to return home with her. Dolly accepts her offer. However, soon after she moves back home, Dolly dies of a stroke. When Riley marries the girl Collin has fallen for, Collin decides to become a lawyer. Before leaving, he and Judge Cool go to River Wood. Collin repeats what Dolly said about the Indian grass speaking. They hear the sound: "It was a grass harp, gathering, telling, a harp of voices remembering a story."

Analysis. Some critics consider the final chapter of this short novel a letdown. Capote himself said the climax of the story occurs when the group comes down from the tree and that the rest of the action sustains the mood of the story. In fact, a sense of closure develops for each of the characters and weaves the narrative into a circle. The novel opens and closes at River Wood. Between these two scenes, Capote enlivens his story with comedy, sadness, and sober reflection. He encircles the whole drama with a halo of mystery, reinforced by the sound of bells tolling and thunder crashing.

Symbolism plays a large part in giving this tale meaning. The river in which Collin and Riley swim suggests not only the flow of time but also a baptism. The tree house is an ark that carries the small group of wayfarers to a new land of discovery. The lush wood where Dolly finds her special herbs is reminiscent of the primordial forest that harbors unfathomable secrets and inscrutable powers. The attic to which Collin retreats symbolizes the decayed past, as well as the secret perch from which he explores the world. It symbolizes, too, the confined, narrow world of his youth, which he must leave in order to become fully an adult. His emergence from that small place symbolizes his entry into the larger world. The circular design of the story eventually brings Collin back to the place where it began, but when it does, he is changed, and ready to leap into the next circle.

SOURCES FOR FURTHER STUDY

Garson, Helen S. *Truman Capote: A Study of the Short Fiction*. New York: Twayne Publishers, 1992.

Goad, Craig M. *Daylight and Darkness, Dream and Delusion: The Works of Truman Capote*. Emporia, Kans.: Emporia State Research Studies, 1967.

Malin, Irving. "From Gothic to Camp." In *The Critical Response to Truman Capote*, edited by Joseph Waldmeir and John Christian. Westport, Conn.: Greenwood Press, 1999.

Moates, Marianne M. (Marianne Merrill). *A Bridge of Childhood: Truman Capote's Southern Years*. New York: H. Holt, 1989.

IN COLD BLOOD

Genre: Novel
Subgenre: Reportorial fiction
Published: New York, 1966
Time period: 1959–1965
Setting: Kansas; Mexico; Florida

Themes and Issues. Although on the surface this story is about crime, punishment, and human depravity and its consequences, Capote is interested in larger meanings as well. He presents the Clutter family as innocents devoured by an evil force—represented by their killers—that is all the more horrible and frightening because it cannot be understood fully.

Capote examines the lives and probes the minds of the murderers to discover what drove them to commit this crime. After six years of research, he had thousands of pages filled with facts, but he had no answer to the central question of why innocent people sometimes fall victim to brutal murder. He implies that evil swims through the world like a marauding shark, an amoral force with no aim other than to act. Some people, such as Dick Hickock and Perry Smith, become its instruments; some, like the Clutters, become its victims. Perhaps this way of thinking led Capote finally to consider the killers themselves victims, destroyed by the same force that caused them to destroy the Clutters.

The central theme is that good and evil are terms people use to explain the inexplicable. Misfortune is a human concept, but humans inhabit a universe that is blind to human suffering, indifferent to human reasoning, and beyond human understanding.

The Plot. Perry Smith and Dick Hickock, ex-convicts who met in the Kansas State Penitentiary, have concocted a scheme to get a great deal of money quickly: They plan to drive to Holcomb, Kansas, and to rob a wealthy wheat farmer, Herb Clutter, who lives with his wife, sixteen-year-old daughter, and fourteen-year-old son. Herb Clutter keeps a safe full of money, according to Dick's former cell mate. To ensure that they leave no witnesses, Dick and Perry plan to tie up their victims and kill each one "in cold blood."

As the Clutter family is shown concluding another typical day, Dick and Perry speed by car toward Holcomb. Arriving just before midnight, the killers wait until the lights in the house go out, then they enter through an unlocked door, tie up each of the Clutters, separate them, make them comfortable, then shoot each one in the head with a shotgun. Searching the house, they find no safe, only forty dollars in Herb's wallet and a silver dollar. Dick and Perry escape to Mexico, then, out of money, they return to Kansas, where they quickly cash some bad checks and set out for Florida.

Meanwhile, the townspeople of Holcomb are shocked, mystified, and frightened by the grisly crime. A team of detectives from the Kansas Bureau of Investigation, headed by Alvin Dewey, begins to investigate but gets nowhere. The killers, again out of money, head back to Kansas, stealing a car along the way, but they are apprehended in Las Vegas, Nevada. Returned to Holcomb by Dewey and his partner, Dick and Perry are tried, convicted, and sentenced to hang. Six years pass before the executions are carried out.

Analysis. *In Cold Blood* benefits from Capote's screenwriting experience. Many of the novel's episodes are laid out using various cinematic techniques. It is as though a camera follows Perry Smith roaming through the Clutter house on the night of the killings. Many other scenes

In René Magritte's *The Empire of Lights* (oil on canvas, 1965) a shadowy figure stands cut off not only from the viewer but from the inviting glow of the windows. The nighttime scene capped by a daytime sky suggests the uneasy tension between light and dark, good and evil, present in Capote's work.

are staged like those in a film, including those in the diner in Olathe, in the garage where Dick works, and in the detective's interview with Dick's family. Capote's eye is the camera, and his descriptions provide lighting. The alternating viewpoint between that of the killers and that of the Clutters not only creates suspense but also establishes contrast, lending each scene a power greater than it would have in a linear sequence. Capote also presents the characters as a director would, each shown in a telling or typical action carefully chosen to arouse the desired emotion in the reader. Dialogue, too, is skillfully used to color a scene or reveal character. One need only note the differences between what is said in Holcomb's diner, at the post office, and in the Clutter home to recognize the way Capote uses dialogue to sculpt character and arouse certain feelings.

By casting the two killers as seedy, calculating, and sly plotters of four grisly murders, Capote lends the book a gothic element. The view of the dark world inhabited by Dick Hickock and Perry Smith increases the perceived luminosity of the Clutter world, with its well-scrubbed morality, precisely tuned schedule, and marblelike sheen. Capote pits these two forces against each other, giving the book the feel of mythic conflict and the characters a larger-than-life significance.

The subtlety of Capote's artistry is nowhere more evident and successful than in the way he transforms a sordid pair of common killers and a good but ordinary family into figures of universal significance. The significance grows implicitly as the narrative advances, gripping the reader with the chill hand of suspense and the sure grasp of certitude. The novel's structure naturally lends itself to filming, but for some viewers the film version that was produced in 1967 seems uninspired. Capote's evocative prose could not be successfully translated into film, and to film the surface is to miss the depths and resonances of his work.

SOURCES FOR FURTHER STUDY

Creeger, George R. *Animals in Exile: Imagery and Theme in Capote's "In Cold Blood."* Middletown, Conn.: Center for Advanced Studies, Wesleyan University, 1967.

Garrett, George. "Crime and Punishment in Kansas: Truman Capote's *In Cold Blood*." *The Hollins Critic* 3, no. 1 (February 1966): 1–12.

Hollowell, John. "Truman Capote's 'Nonfiction Novel.'" In *Fact and Fiction: The New Journalism and the Nonfiction Novel.* Chapel Hill: University of North Carolina Press, 1977.

Malin, Irving, ed. *Truman Capote's "In Cold Blood": A Critical Handbook.* Belmont, Calif.: Wadsworth, 1968.

With its powerful blend of fact and fiction, *In Cold Blood* brought a shocking realism to the American novel. The nonfiction novel gave Capote the freedom to probe the roots of senseless brutality and inexplicable violence. The film adaptation, which starred actor Robert Blake as Perry Smith (above center), was released in 1967, just a year after the publication of the novel.

Other Works

THE DOGS BARK: PUBLIC PEOPLE AND PRIVATE PLACES (1973). A collection of fiction and nonfiction, this book represents the broad range of Truman Capote's interests and writing skills from the beginning of his publishing career to the decade before his death. This miscellany ideally suits Capote's intellectual and artistic gifts, for it offers an array of vivid descriptions of out-of-the-way locales, absorbing portraiture, and lively commentary on people and places. Although it lacks both the plot continuity and character of fiction, Capote unifies the whole with his constant presence as the eye through which his subjects are viewed. The reader is carried along by his graceful prose and rich descriptive detail, as entirely absorbed by Capote's subject as the author is.

MUSIC FOR CHAMELEONS (1980). Capote's final complete work was another miscellany, this one collecting some of his last writings. He enjoyed writing short pieces, which did not require much time and did not have to meet the high standards that a full-length novel did, especially one that would compete with *In Cold Blood*. These short pieces, however, contain some of his best, most mature, writing. In

René Magritte's *Le Faux Miroir (The False Mirror)* reflects the penetrating attention Capote gives to fine detail. His rich descriptions, particularly in *The Dogs Bark* and *In Cold Blood*, suggest that there is little, if anything, that clouds his vision.

them, Capote relaxes, experimenting with subjects and techniques. In "A Day's Work," he tags along with a cleaning woman on some of her jobs. The narrative is absorbing reading, as the woman provides a running commentary on her employers. Capote even manages a climactic episode in which the woman confronts two of her employers and comes out a winner.

The centerpiece of the book, however, is "Handcarved Coffins," whose subtitle describes the work's nature: "A Nonfiction Account of an American Crime." Capote boasted that he had invented yet another art form, pointing toward the future of the novel. Critics quickly dismissed this claim, but the work won praise for its tightly controlled handling of a blend of fact and fiction. The down-to-earth detective who investigates the case is not a real character, but rather a fictional portrait of several people Capote knew.

The piece combines dialogue and descriptive prose as the story line follows the efforts of a detective, Jake Pepper, to arrest a Nebraska rancher, Bob Quinn, suspected of killing not only one of his wives but also several people who tried to divert a river from his property. Suspense mounts as the murders increase in number and inventiveness, with methods such as liquid nicotine, decapitation, and rattlesnakes. All the while, the charming, sociable Quinn maintains a good-natured facade that is never proven to be just a facade.

OTHER VOICES, OTHER ROOMS (1948). The protagonist of this dark tale is thirteen-year-old Joel Harrison Knox, who, after his mother dies, comes to live with his father. He arrives in Noon City, a town near his father's plantation and is met by Jesus Fever, an old black retainer who takes Joel to his father's house, Skully's Landing. Joel is not allowed to see his father, who remains mysteriously hidden in a darkened room. Joel's stepmother also lives in the house, along with her cousin, Randolph, who, in his mid-thirties, goes about in silk pajamas and kimonos.

Other strange characters inhabit the fringes of this dreamlike world, including the dwarflike Jesus Fever; Jesus's granddaughter, Zoo, who bears a scar on her neck from the wound her bridegroom gave her on their wedding night; and Little Sunshine, a black hermit who lives in an abandoned resort. Joel's father is a paralyzed and almost speechless recluse who communicates by bouncing red tennis balls onto the floor from his bed. Eerie events occur from the beginning of the novel. One day, for example, Joel sees what looks like a woman's ghostly face looking down at him from a window. The woman is wearing a towering white wig.

When Joel learns that Randolph, not his father, wrote to invite him to Skully's Landing, he feels betrayed and runs away but catches pneumonia and returns. Nursed back to health by Randolph, he realizes he cannot run away. Skully's Landing is where he belongs. At this moment of discovery, the strange face reappears in the window and beckons to him. Joel, finally seeing that it is Randolph, knows that he must go to him. Unafraid and wise with self-realization, he leaves behind the boy he was.

The novel's unrealistic setting, characters, and events underscore the allegorical nature of the story. The fantastic figures have the distorted features of a mind searching for understanding. Allegorically, the story depicts a son in search of his father, but the psychological focus is on Joel's maturation and self-discovery. The haunting figures on the fringes symbolize the unknown that lurks beyond understanding, yet they also offer companionship and social support. The nature of Joel's world is defined by the desire to escape, the fear of strangeness, and the darkness of surrounding ignorance.

Capote's surrealism charms as it enchants; his figures prove to be likable eccentrics, not monsters. The psychological and moral center of the tale is Randolph, the benevolent companion, whose bizarre behavior is more endearing than threatening. Joel's self-possession reassures us that the darkness is less dangerous than it appears. In the end, Joel is comfortable in this carnival world, and it is clear that it will not devour him.

In Robert Gwathmey's oil painting *Reflections* (Morris Museum of Art, Augusta, Georgia), painted around 1950, a figure stares into a mirror, perplexed by the distorted image staring back at her. Many of Capote's characters undergo the same painful self-scrutiny in their struggle for identity and understanding.

Resources

The New York Public Library houses a collection of Truman Capote's papers from 1924 to 1984, which includes letters, photos, and manuscripts. Other sources of interest to Capote readers include:

Interviews. Capote was considered a superb conversationalist, and several recordings illustrate the point. Although some of Capote's conversations were first broadcast on television, they are available only on audiotape. On *The Dinah Shore Show* (January 21,

1976), Capote describes the characteristics of a good writer, his auditory vision, and photographic memory. In an interview for PBS-TV (March 14, 1983), Capote talks about the origins of his writing career, his anxieties, his friendship with Tennessee Williams, and his homosexuality. Capote may also be heard reading his short story "A Christmas Memory" (Chicago: Beverly Records and Costumes, 1996).

Videos. Capote was the subject of a television biography by Deirdre O'Hearn and Edward Herrmann, titled

Truman Capote: The Tiny Terror, for the A&E television network (distributed by New Video Group, 1997). He also is the subject of *Truman Capote*, another audiovisual record (Detroit: Gale Research, 1971). Perhaps the most entertaining of this kind of material is titled *Gore Vidal Describes and Decimates Norman Mailer, Truman Capote, Presidents Kennedy, Johnson, Eisenhower, and Nixon, Does Imitations of JFK, Ike, and FDR, and Discusses His Own Homosexuality*, broadcast on the CBS television network on July 27, 1975.

Truman Capote: Links. This excellent Web site offers links to information about Capote, to the New York Public Library, to booksellers of his books, and to a film database. (http://www.ansoniadesign.com/capote/links.htm)

BERNARD E. MORRIS

Raymond Carver

BORN: May 25, 1938, Clatskanie, Oregon
DIED: August 2, 1988, Port Angeles, Washington
IDENTIFICATION: Perhaps the most important American short-fiction writer of the 1970s and 1980s, his works sparked a renaissance of interest in the short story as a literary form.

Raymond Carver's first two major collections of short stories, *Will You Please Be Quiet, Please?* (1976) and *What We Talk About When We Talk About Love* (1981), fascinated readers with their cryptic, economical prose style and their focus on puzzling disruptions in the lives of everyday people. His characters seem caught in emotional traps they can neither escape nor understand. Unable to find engaging work, meaningful relationships, or fulfilling lives, they drift, drink, and struggle to understand why they do what they do and what they want. Carver's characters seem real in a gritty everyday way, but they also seem somehow dreamlike and beyond reality, thus earning Carver's unique style and vision the term "hyperrealism."

The Writer's Life

Raymond Carver was born on May 25, 1938, in Clatskanie, a small town in northwestern Oregon to Clevie Raymond and Ella Casey Carver. In 1941, his family moved to Yakima, Washington, where his father worked as a logger. There Carver received his education through high school.

The Future Writer. Carver said that growing up in the rural Pacific Northwest, where he spent much of his youth hunting and fishing, made him want to be a "writer from the West." He once told an interviewer that he could not remember when he did not want to be a writer; he even took a correspondence course in writing when he was a teenager. As a young man his literary tastes were typical and unassuming. He read the westerns of Zane Gray, the science fiction of Edgar Rice Burroughs, and men's magazines such as *True*, *Argosy*, *Sports Afield*, and *Outdoor Life*—a reading list that may partially account for the relatively plain style of his short stories and for his simple plot structures.

Fatherhood, echoed in this photograph of a man with children, left little time for Carver to write long fiction. As a result, he spent much of his free time mastering the short story.

Carver married Maryann Burk in 1957, when he was nineteen; his first child, Christine LaRae, was born a few months later. Carver and his new family moved to Paradise, California, in 1958, where he entered Chico State College. His son, Vance Lindsay, was born the following year. Carver later declared that the most important influence on his early hopes to become a writer was the fact that he married and became a father before he was twenty. The pressures of supporting his young family made it almost impossible for him to find time to write. He turned to the short story form because it was the best suited to the circumstances of his life. Even though he revised extensively, he knew that he could finish a draft for a short story within a few sittings.

Early Influences and Struggles. Carver said that the most important positive influence on his career while at Chico State College was his enrollment in a creative writing class taught by John Gardner, who would later be known for such novels as *Grendel* (1971), *The Sunlight Dialogues* (1972), and *October Light* (1976), as well as for nonfiction and criticism. Carver compared Gardner to the great artistic and literary masters of the past, who nurtured their apprentices. Because of Gardner, Carver began to consider writing a high calling, something to be taken very seriously. In 1960 he transferred to Humboldt State University on the Northern California coast, where he studied under short-story writer Richard Day and published his own first stories. He received his bachelor's degree from Humboldt State in 1963.

After his story "Pastoral" was published in *Western Humanities Review* in 1963, Carver left for the

Iowa Writers' Workshop at the University of Iowa with a small graduate grant of five hundred dollars. However, unable to write and still support his family, he returned to California before the end of the academic year. Carver held a number of minor jobs in Sacramento, as a mill hand and a delivery person, but perhaps his most fortunate job was a two-year stint as a night watchman at a hospital, where he was able to squeeze in writing time. In 1967 Carver took a position as a textbook editor for Science Research Associates in Palo Alto, California.

Initial Success.

A key milestone in Carver's career was the selection of his story "Will You Please Be Quiet, Please?" for the 1967 edition of *The Best American Short Stories*. Another important event in his life as a writer occurred the following year when the English Club at Sacramento State College published twenty-six of his poems in a collection entitled *Near Klamath*. Although Carver was busy writing during the 1960s and publishing his poetry and fiction in various small magazines, his biggest break came in 1970 when he was fired from his Science Research Associates job and received a National Endowment for the Arts Discovery Award for Poetry. With money from the grant, unemployment benefits, and severance pay, he found the time to write and revise many of his stories. Carver was soon publishing in reputable journals and well-paying magazines, such as *Esquire* and *Harper's Bazaar*.

From 1971 to 1972, Carver taught at the University of California, Santa Cruz, and in the fall of 1972 he held a Wallace Stegner Fellowship in creative writing at Stanford University. During the fall semester of 1973, he also had a visiting writers' appointment at the Iowa Writers' Workshop. His story "Put Yourself in My Shoes" appeared in the 1974 edition of *O. Henry Prize Stories*, and the following year "Are You a Doctor?" was chosen for the 1975 *O. Henry Prize Stories*. He published *Will You Please Be Quiet, Please?*, his first book of stories, as well as a collection of poems, *At Night the Salmon Move*, in 1976. The following year *Will You Please Be Quiet, Please?* was nominated for the National Book Award.

Alcoholism and a Crucial Turning Point.

As Carver gained broader recognition for his work, he was also suffering from alcoholism. He admitted that he and his colleague, the well-known writer John Cheever, were drinking so heavily during their tenure at the Iowa Writers' Workshop that they did not once take the covers off their typewriters while they were there. In 1977 Carver was hospitalized several times, and in the following year he separated from his wife, Maryann.

However, on June 2, 1977, his Alcoholics Anonymous "birth date," Carver stopped drinking for good, and both his personal and professional life began to brighten. He received a Guggenheim Fellowship in 1977 and a National Endowment for the Arts grant in 1979. In 1980 he was appointed a professor of English at Syracuse University. He published the highly praised collection of stories *What We Talk About When We Talk About Love* in 1981 and his third important story collection, *Cathedral*, in 1983.

Carver's gravestone in Ocean View Cemetery, west of Port Angeles, Washington. Carver's death from lung cancer came at a time when he had found happiness in both his personal and professional life.

HIGHLIGHTS IN CARVER'S LIFE

1938 Raymond Carver is born on May 25 in Clatskanie, Oregon.

1941 Moves to Yakima, Washington.

1957 Marries Maryann Burk; daughter, Christine LaRae, is born.

1958 Moves with wife and daughter to Paradise, California; enters Chico State College; studies creative writing with John Gardner.

1960 Transfers to Humboldt State University in Northern California.

1963 Graduates from Humboldt State; enters Iowa Writers' Workshop at the University of Iowa.

1967 His short story "Will You Please Be Quiet, Please?" is selected for *The Best American Short Stories*.

1968 Carver publishes *Near Klamath*, a book of poems.

1972 Receives Wallace Stegner Fellowship in creative writing at Stanford University.

1976 Publishes short-story collection *Will You Please Be Quiet, Please?* and a book of poems, *At Night the Salmon Move*.

1977 Awarded Guggenheim Fellowship; *Will You Please Be Quiet, Please?* is nominated for National Book Award.

1978 Meets Tess Gallagher.

1979 Receives National Endowment for the Arts Fellowship.

1981 Publishes *What We Talk About When We Talk About Love*, a book of stories.

1982 Divorces Maryann Carver.

1983 Publishes *Cathedral*; is nominated for National Book Critics Circle Award and a Pulitzer Prize; receives Mildred and Harold Strauss Living Award.

1988 Publishes book of stories, *Where I'm Calling From*; marries Tess Gallagher on June 17; dies of lung cancer on August 2, in Port Angeles, Washington.

1989 *A New Path to the Waterfall* is published posthumously.

Career Peaks and Final Tragedy. In 1982 Carver divorced his wife, Maryann, and continued living with Tess Gallagher, a fellow writer who remained his companion from 1978 until his death. In 1983 he was awarded the Mildred and Harold Strauss Living Award, a five-year grant of thirty-five thousand dollars a year. He published three volumes of poetry, *Where Water Comes Together with Other Water* (1985), *Ultramarine* (1986), and *In a Marine Light* (1987) in Great Britain.

However, in 1987, after he had gathered another collection of stories, Carver, a heavy smoker, was diagnosed with lung cancer. He underwent surgery in the fall and radiation treatments afterward, but his condition had already progressed too far. He died in Port Angeles, Washington, on August 2, 1988. His final collection of stories, *Where I'm Calling From*, was published that same year. His last collection of poetry, *A New Path to the Waterfall*, was published posthumously in 1989.

The Writer's Work

Raymond Carver was first and foremost a short-story writer. The twenty-two stories in his first collection, *Will You Please Be Quiet, Please?*, are startling in their unsettling images of ordinary working-class people caught in comic helplessness and unarticulated desperation. Carver's characters are, often for seemingly trivial and baffling reasons, thrown out of their everyday routine and into situations where they feel helpless and estranged. Carver's hyperrealistic descriptions of ordinary objects create an overall hallucinatory effect.

Style and Themes. The stories in Carver's second major collection, *What We Talk About When We Talk About Love*, recall the styles of two of his most important predecessors—Anton Chekhov and Ernest Hemingway—and are even more radically economical and elliptical. Most of these stories would later appear in *Where I'm Calling From* in longer original versions reinstated by Carver. The stories' themes are suggested as much by the bare outlines of their sometimes shocking and sometimes trivial events as by the spare dialogue of their characters, who seem utterly unable to account for their actions or to articulate the nature of their isolation. The characters have either first names or no names at all. They are so briefly described that they seem to have no physical presence; at the same time they seem absolutely ordinary.

Carver's Characters. The characters in Carver's stories often have too little money and too much to drink; they have trouble holding jobs and trouble holding their marriages together. However, Carver does not focus on cultural and economic problems that can be solved by social reform. Rather, Carver's characters seem caught up in mysterious forces beyond their control and beyond their power of explanation. The most basic theme of Carver's stories is the tenuous union between men and women and the mysterious separations that always seem to threaten them.

However, the stories that appear in Carver's collections *Cathedral* and *Where I'm Calling From* are more optimistic and hopeful than his earlier stories, perhaps because they were mainly written after he had stopped drinking and had met Tess Gallagher. These stories are longer and more detailed, as Carver and his narrators seem more willing and able to discuss, explain, and explore the emotions and situations that haunt them. These later pieces, characterized by a mood of reconciliation and calm self-awareness and acceptance, move toward union or reunion. This shift resulted in a more conventional short-story form than Carver had previously employed.

This still from *Short Cuts*, a movie based on several of Carver's short stories, imbues the comic helplessness Carver's characters experience when an ordinary situation somehow becomes absurd.

Raymond Carver himself said that nothing influenced his work as much as the fact that he married young, had a family early in life, and had to work at menial jobs rather than devote time to his writing. The fact that Carver focused his attention on the short story and poetry rather than on the more popular novelistic form can be partially attributed to the fact that he had to steal small amounts of writing time whenever he could.

The most important authors to influence Carver's writing were Anton Chekhov and Ernest Hemingway. Carver frequently noted his debt to Chekhov for his highly polished prose and his ordinary characters confronting seemingly trivial everyday disasters. Although Carver gave less credit to Hemingway for his subject matter and style, many critics have noted the similarity between Carver's early works' laconic and seemingly simple prose style and that of Hemingway.

The teacher and editor who most influenced Carver was John Gardner, his first creative-writing teacher at Chico State College. Carver praised Gardner's inspiration and encouragement in his early efforts to learn to write. Gardner was the first "real" writer Carver had met, and he contributed to Carver's own desire to be a writer. Another writer who had a profound influence on Carver was Richard Day, who taught Carver at Humboldt State University. Day became Carver's good friend and helped him get published. He was also influential in Carver's first visit to the famous Iowa Writers' Workshop at the University of Iowa.

Another important influence was the author and editor Gordon Lish, who, as editor of *Esquire* magazine, introduced Carver's work to a broader audience. Lish was also instrumental in the publication of Carver's first book. Lish's editing of some of Carver's earlier stories also contributed to Carver's early style.

Finally, two of the most important influences on Carver's career were his renunciation of alcohol and his relationship and editorial mutuality with the writer Tess Gallagher, who became his constant companion and colleague in his final years. Carver's sobriety and his new life with Gallagher perhaps had much to do with themes of hope and reconciliation in his last works.

These oil-on-canvas portraits of Carver and Carver's wife, Tess Gallagher, are a loving tribute from their friend, Mexican artist Alfredo Arreguin. Carver's portrait, titled *Ray's Ghost Fish*, reflects Carver's desire to go fishing, which he expressed to Arreguin after undergoing a chemotherapy treatment. The birds adorning Gallagher's portrait, *Our Lady of Poetry*, delighted her because they reminded her of Carver's poem "Hummingbird," one of the last poems he wrote for her.

SHORT FICTION

1974	Put Yourself in My Shoes
1976	Will You Please Be Quiet, Please?
1977	Furious Seasons and Other Stories
1981	What We Talk About When We Talk About Love
1983	Cathedral
1983	Fires
1988	Elephant and Other Stories
1988	Where I'm Calling From

POETRY

1968	Near Klamath
1970	Winter Insomnia
1976	At Night the Salmon Move
1982	Two Poems
1985	This Water
1985	Where Water Comes Together with Other Water
1986	Ultramarine
1987	In a Marine Light (Great Britain)
1989	A New Path to the Waterfall
1996	All Of Us: The Collected Poems

MISCELLANEOUS

1983	Fires: Essays, Poems, Stories
1990	Carver Country: The World of Raymond Carver
1991	No Heroics, Please: Uncollected Writings
2000	Call If You Need Me: The Uncollected Fiction and Other Prose

FILMS BASED ON CARVER'S WORKS

1987	Feathers
1993	Short Cuts
1995	Autumn of the Leaves

Carver's Legacy. Raymond Carver is the most important figure in the 1980s renaissance of short fiction in American literature. Indeed, the popularity of his stories is the single-most important source of this renaissance. He was in the forefront of a short-fiction trend during this period that author John Barth playfully termed "hyperrealistic minimalism," or the "less-is-more" school. Carver himself never accepted the term *minimalism* as an accurate description of his work because he felt it failed to convey the complexity of his stories. As far as Carver was concerned, his writing was not the result of minimalistic ambitions but the opposite, a desire for his exactness to cause what he wrote to reverberate, thereby giving his expression a stronger effect. Like the stories of Chekhov and Hemingway, Carver's stories communicate indirectly, suggesting much but saying little.

Carver's understanding of the merits of the short-story form and his sensitivity to the situations of modern men and women caught in tenuous relationships and inexplicable separations have made him a sympathetic spokesperson for those who cannot articulate their own dilemmas. Although critics disagree about the relative merits of Carver's early experimental stories versus his later, morally optimistic stories, most agree with the general opinion that Raymond Carver is the ultimate modern master of the short-story form.

BIBLIOGRAPHY

Campbell, Ewing. *Raymond Carver: A Study of the Short Fiction.* New York: Twayne Publishers, 1992.

Ford, Richard. "Good Raymond." *The New Yorker* 74 (October 5, 1998): 70–79.

Gentry, Marshall Bruce, and William L. Stuff, eds. *Conversations with Raymond Carver.* Jackson: University of Mississippi Press, 1990.

Halpert, Saul, ed. *Raymond Carver: An Oral Biography.* Iowa City: University of Iowa Press, 1995.

Kelly, Lionel. "Anton Chekhov and Raymond Carver: A Writer's Strategies of Reading." *Yearbook of English Studies* 26 (1996): 218–231.

Meyer, Adam. *Raymond Carver.* New York: Twayne Publishers, 1995.

Nesset, Kirk. *The Stories of Raymond Carver.* Athens: Ohio University Press, 1995.

Runyon, Randolph Paul. *Reading Raymond Carver.* Syracuse, N.Y.: Syracuse University Press, 1992.

Salzman, Arthur M. *Understanding Raymond Carver.* Columbia: University of South Carolina Press, 1988.

Stull, William L. "Raymond Carver." *Dictionary of Literary Biography Yearbook*: 1988 (Detroit: Gale Research, 1989): 199–213.

Stull, and Maureen P. Carroll. *Remembering Ray: A Composite Biography of Raymond Carver,* Santa Barbara: Capra Press, 1993.

Reader's Guide to Major Works

"A SMALL, GOOD THING" ("THE BATH")
   Genre: Short story
   Subgenre: Domestic tragedy
   Published: New York, 1981 (republished in 1983)
   Time period: 1970s
   Setting: American suburbia

Themes and Issues. "The Bath" originally appeared in *What We Talk About When We Talk About Love* and then appeared in its initial form as "A Small Good Thing" in both *Cathedral* and *Where I'm Calling From*. The first published version depicts a mysterious invasion of everyday life, while the second version explores the effect of a child's death on a suburban couple and how the two finally manage to reaffirm human hope and communion.

The Plot. Both versions of the story focus on a couple whose son is hit by a car on his eighth birthday and is hospitalized in a coma. In both versions, the couple receive annoying anonymous phone calls from a baker from whom the wife had earlier ordered a custom-made birthday cake. However, "The Bath," told in Raymond Carver's earlier style, is less concerned with the couple's personal feelings about the persistent anonymous calls than with the mysterious and perverse interruption of the calls themselves.

Analysis. "A Small, Good Thing" is five times longer than "The Bath" because it sympathetically explores the emotional life of the couple, suggesting that their son's situation binds them together in a way in which they have never been united before. Whereas in "The Bath," the child's death abruptly ends the story, in "A Small, Good Thing," the couple discover that it is the baker who has been calling and visit him after the boy's death. He shares their sorrow;

Nighthawks, a 1942 oil-on-canvas painting by artist Edward Hopper (1882–1967). Hopper's ability to isolate characters, even when they are in the company of others, appealed to Carver, whose own work often reflects the strange intimacy of being together and alone at the same time.

they share his loneliness. The story ends with a reconciliation in the warm and comfortable bakery as the couple, in a ritual of breaking bread together, eat and talk into the early morning, not wanting to leave—as if their sharing marks the true nature of healing sympathy and identification.

The difference between "The Bath" and "A Small, Good Thing" provides a striking example of how Carver's writing style and thematic concerns changed in the middle of his career. Whereas "The Bath" is about a mysterious invasion into everyday life, "A Small, Good Thing" is an exploration of human reconciliation and emotional acceptance.

SOURCES FOR FURTHER STUDY

Campbell, Ewing. *Raymond Carver: A Study of the Short Fiction*. New York: Twayne Publishers, 1992.

Meyer, Adam. *Raymond Carver*. New York: Twayne Publishers, 1995.

Salzman, Arthur M. *Understanding Raymond Carver*. Columbia: University of South Carolina Press, 1988

Stull, William L. "Beyond Hopelessville: Another Side of Raymond Carver." *Philological Quarterly* 64 (Winter 1985): 1–15.

"CATHEDRAL"

Genre: Short story
Subgenre: Psychological realism
Published: New York, 1983
Time period: 1970s
Setting: Suburban home

Themes and Issues. The title story of Carver's third collection is the most emphatic indicator of the shift in Carver's technique and thematic concerns after his own personal life became more stabilized. The story contains much more exposition and background than the stories in Carver's first, more cryptic, collections.

The Plot. "Cathedral" is told by a cynical and skeptical man who resents that an old friend of his wife—a blind man for whom the wife once read—has come to visit. The conversation between the narrator, his wife, and the blind man is mainly devoted to the blind man dispelling many of the narrator's prejudiced ideas about the blind.

The most significant encounter between the narrator and the blind man begins when, while watching a television program about the Church in the Middle Ages, the blind man asks the narrator to find some paper and a pen so that they can draw a cathedral together. The blind man puts his hand over the hand of the narrator and tells him to draw with the blind man's hand following along with him. When they finish, the blind man asks the narrator to look at the drawing and tell him what he thinks, but the narrator keeps his eyes closed. He knows that he is in his house, but he says he didn't feel like he was inside anything. "It's really something," he says.

Analysis. "Cathedral" is a much-admired Carver story, often discussed in university literature classes. It marks a turning point through the emotional catharsis in its ending, which enacts a classic epiphany much like stories such as James Joyce's "The Dead." The narrator reaches an understanding at the end that allows him to identify with the blind man, but beyond that we also feel the spiritual transformation of the narrator as he connects with cosmic dimensions beyond observable and everyday phenomena. Also, the reader is invited to join the narrator in his spiritual opening, through the very accomplishment of epiphany.

SOURCES FOR FURTHER STUDY

Bugeja. "Tarnish and Silver: An Analysis of Carver's *Cathedral*." *The South Dakota Review* 24 (Autumn 1986): 73–87.

Cushman, Keith. "Blind, Intertextual Love: 'The Blind Man' and Raymond Carver's 'Cathedral.' In *D. H. Lawrence's Literary Inheritors*. New York: St. Martin's Press, 1991.

Facknitz, Mark A. R. "'The Calm,' 'A Small, Good Thing,' and 'Cathedral': Raymond Carver and the Rediscovery of Human Worth." *Studies in Short Fiction* 23 (Summer 1986): 287–296.

Nesset, Kirk. *The Stories of Raymond Carver*. Athens: Ohio University Press, 1995.

"ERRAND"

Genre: Short story
Subgenre: Historical realism
Published: New York, 1988
Time period: July 2, 1904
Setting: Badenweiler, Germany

Themes and Issues. "Errand" was published not long before Carver's death, when he knew he had cancer, and deals with the death of one of Carver's mentors, Anton Chekhov. It serves as a kind of farewell tribute to the great short-story writer.

The Plot. Most of the story reads very much like a straightforward account of Chekhov's death in a hotel in the resort city of Badenweiler, Germany. The story recounts Chekhov's last hours while a doctor visits him in his room and his wife, Olga Knipper, stands by helplessly. Knowing that Chekhov will be dead in a matter of minutes, the doctor orders champagne and three glasses from the kitchen. A few minutes after taking a drink, Chekhov dies. Later, a young waiter returns to the room to bring a vase of roses and to retrieve the champagne bottle and glasses. Olga Knipper, who has spent the remainder of the night sitting alone with Chekhov's body, sends the waiter into the town to find a mortician, someone who takes great pains in his work and whose manner is appropriately reserved.

The young man listens as Olga tells him that he should behave as if he is engaged on a great errand, moving down the sidewalk as if he were carrying in his arms a porcelain vase of roses that he has to deliver to an important man. Meanwhile, the boy is thinking of something else; on the previous night, just after Chekhov died, the cork that the doctor had pushed back into the champagne bottle popped out again and now lies just at the toe of the boy's shoe. When Olga finishes describing the errand she wishes the boy to perform, he leans over and, without looking, closes the cork into his hand.

Analysis. Olga Knipper's highly detailed, storylike instructions to the young waiter and the single, simple detail of his bending over to pick up the cork make "Errand" a story rather than a mere historical report and thus a fitting tribute to the art of short-story writing, which both Chekhov and Carver pursued. As Olga tells the boy what must happen, the events seem magically to have already happened, as she instills a story in his mind. The cork is not symbolic of anything; it is a concrete object in the world that one can almost tangibly feel when the boy closes his hand around it. It fulfills Chekhov's insistence that if a gun is described hanging on a wall early in a story, then it must be fired before the end; more important, it embodies the most crucial lesson that Carver learned from Chekhov—that human meaning is communicated by the simplest of gestures and the most trivial of objects.

The Russian writer Anton Chekhov (1860–1904). Chekhov's death was the subject of Carver's short story "Errand," which was written not long before Carver's own death. Chekhov's short stories, with their mundane characters and their outwardly insignificant dilemmas, greatly influenced Carver.

SOURCES FOR FURTHER STUDY

Kelly, Lionel. "Anton Chekhov and Raymond Carver: A Writer's Strategies of Reading." *Yearbook of English Studies* 26 (1996): 218–231.

Nesset, Kirk. *The Stories of Raymond Carver*. Athens: Ohio University Press, 1995.

Runyon, Randolph Paul. *Reading Raymond Carver*. Syracuse, N.Y.: Syracuse University Press, 1992.

"NEIGHBORS"

Genre: Short story
Subgenre: Psychological realism
Published: New York, 1976
Time period:
    1960s
Setting: American
    suburbia

Themes and Issues. The mysterious fascination that two people have in prowling around their neighbors' apartment when they are out of town provides the basis for this eerie exploration of a universal human desire to live the life of someone else.

The Plot. "Neighbors" focuses on Bill and Arlene Miller, a couple who feels that their neighbors, Jim and Harriet Stone, lead fuller lives than they do. The Stones ask the Millers to look after their apartment and water their plants while they are away on vacation. When Bill goes to the Stones' apartment, he begins to take trivial things from it, such as a container of pills and some cigarettes. He eats food and drinks whiskey and stays longer at the apartment than he needs to. He secretly takes off from work and slips in to spend the day alone there, first trying on a shirt and Bermuda shorts belonging to Jim and then a brassiere and pair of panties belonging to Harriet.

The story comes to a climax when the reader discovers that Arlene is similarly fascinated with the apartment, telling her husband she found some secret pictures in a bedroom drawer. When the couple try to go back in the apartment and discover they have locked the key inside, they feel desperate.

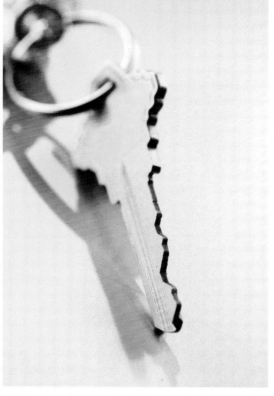

The key to a neighbor's home presents the main characters with the opportunity to fulfill voyeuristic desires in Carver's short story "Neighbors."

Analysis. This is a story about the fascination of visiting someone else's secret inner reality and the excitement of temporarily taking on another identity. It alludes to the universal dissatisfaction that every-one occasionally feels with being merely one's self and the universal inner desire to change places with someone else. Bill's desire to make love to his wife after visiting the apartment reflects the erotic thrill of peeking into someone else's life and then imaginatively fulfilling that fantasy. The desperation that Bill and Arlene feel at the end of the story when they find themselves locked out of the Stones' apartment, bracing themselves as if against a wind, points to the impossibility of truly entering into the lives of others, except temporarily to visit and inevitably to violate.

SOURCES FOR FURTHER STUDY

Campbell, Ewing. *Raymond Carver: A Study of the Short Fiction*. New York: Twayne Publishers, 1992.

Runyon, Randolph Paul. *Reading Raymond Carver*. Syracuse, N.Y.: Syracuse University Press, 1992.

Salzman, Arthur M. *Understanding Raymond Carver*. Columbia: University of South Carolina Press, 1988.

"WHY DON'T YOU DANCE?"

Genre: Short story
Subgenre: Psychological realism
Published: New York, 1981
Time period: 1970s
Setting: Suburban neighborhood

Themes and Issues. When a man's marriage mysteriously comes apart, he externalizes his marriage's inner life. When a young couple just starting out in life enters the man's externalized inner world, the reader senses that life is an eternal circle in which old mismatches are endlessly repeated.

The Plot. The story begins with an unnamed man who has, for no apparent reason, arranged all his furniture out on his front lawn just as it had been oriented in the house; he has even plugged in the television and other appliances so that they work as they did inside. The absence of the man's wife suggests that his marriage has collapsed.

When the man leaves to buy some food and beverages, a young couple, who are furnishing their first apartment, stop and begin to inspect the furniture. When the man returns, the couple make offers for some of the furnishings, and the man indifferently accepts whatever they suggest. The man plays a record on the phonograph, and the boy and the girl—and then the man and the girl—dance. The story ends with a brief epilogue as, weeks later, the girl tells a friend about the incident.

Analysis. By placing all his furniture on his front lawn, the man has revealed what previously has been hidden in the house. The young couple are beginning their marriage as the man is ending his. In buying the man's furniture, they are establishing their own relationship on the remains of the man's.

However, the seemingly minor conflicts between the two young people—the boy's watching television and girl's wanting him to try the bed; her wanting to dance and his drinking—suggest another doomed relationship like the one that has ended. As the girl senses, "there is more to it" than a garage sale, but she cannot articulate the meaning of the event; she can only retell it over and over, trying to understand it.

SOURCES FOR FURTHER STUDY

Campbell, Ewing. *Raymond Carver: A Study of the Short Fiction*. New York: Twayne Publishers, 1992.

Meyer, Adam. *Raymond Carver*. New York: Twayne Publishers, 1995.

Runyon, Randolph Paul. *Reading Raymond Carver*. Syracuse, N.Y.: Syracuse University Press, 1992.

Other Works

"WHAT WE TALK ABOUT WHEN WE TALK ABOUT LOVE" (1981). This is primarily a dialogue story in which two couples meet and drink gin in Albuquerque, New Mexico. Mel and his second wife, Teresa, and the narrator and his wife, Laura, somehow get on the subject of love, during which Mel dominates the conversation with his idea that "real love" is nothing less than spiritual. Teresa tells about a man with whom she once lived, who loved her so much that he drank rat poison and shot himself in the mouth when she left him. However, Mel says he is not interested in that kind of love.

Mel then tells a story of a couple in their seventies who had a car wreck on the interstate that he says should make them all ashamed "when we talk like we know what we're talking about when we talk about love." When both the man and woman are put in casts, with only

The corroded exterior of this dilapidated car, found not far from Carver's birthplace, implies the physical damage an elderly couple sustains in a car accident in Carver's short story "What We Talk About When We Talk About Love."

small holes for their eyes, noses, and mouths, the husband is depressed because he cannot see his wife. "Can you imagine?" Mel insists. "I'm telling you, the man's heart was breaking because he couldn't turn his goddamn head and see his goddamn wife. . . . Do you see what I'm saying?"

The story is a clear example of the frustration of the typical Raymond Carver narrator when trying to tell a story to explain some mysterious aspect of human motivation and behavior. It is also a pure example of Carver's deeply held conviction that when people talk about what is most important to them, they usually rely on story to do so. Rather than trying to explain something in rational terms, Carver's narrator tells a seemingly simple story,

hoping to tell it in such a way that the meaning will be mysteriously and almost intuitively felt.

"WILL YOU PLEASE BE QUIET, PLEASE?"
(1976). Most critics agree that "Will You Please Be Quiet, Please?" is the precursor to Carver's later, more optimistic, stories because it is richer in background information and because it ends in the central character's reconciliation with his unfaithful wife. Carver's central focus in this story is on the universal problem of coping with discoveries for which there is no practical way to prepare.

When the central character, Ralph's wife, Marian, tells him of her past infidelity, he enters into a dazed realm of reality, wandering through his small town envisioning grotesque sexual images. He returns home, and his wife tries to talk to him, but he does not want her explanations and justifications. He wants only to be left alone with his thoughts. He feels impossible changes moving within him, and he must come to terms with this disruption to his seemingly comfortable life. The profound truth that Ralph understands at the end of the story is that there is no way to predict one's own behavior, no way to understand why people do what they do, and no way to prepare for unforeseen events that break up one's expectations about life.

$\mathcal{R}esources$

Sources of interest to students of Raymond Carver include the following:

Carver: The Raymond Carver Web Site. This comprehensive Web site, created by Tom Luce, a student of Tess Gallagher at Whitman College, includes adetailed biography and chronology by William Stull, photographs from Tess Gallagher's album, an essay refuting Carver's so-called minimalism, a list of Carver's favorite childhood books, and even brief recordings of Carver. (http://people.whitman.edu/~lecetb/carver/)

To Write and Keep Kind. This documentary television program, produced by KCTS television for PBS in 1992, features interviews with Carver friends, family, critics, and admirers.

Raymond Carver Interview and Stories with Kay Bonetti. An informative interview with readings by Carver was originally broadcast on National Public Radio in 1983 and is available on audiocassette from American Audio Prose Library.

Audio Recordings. Several of Carver's collections are available on audiocassette, read by others, including *Blackbird Pie and Other Stories* (1992), *Nobody Said Anything and Other Stories* (1992), and *What We Talk About When We Talk About Love* (1992), all from Books in Motion. Readings of Carver's stories appear in the collections *American Masters: The Short Stories of Raymond Carver, John Cheever, and John Updike* (1998), from Random House Audiobooks, and *Great American Writers: Twenty-one Unabridged Stories* (1996), from Audio Partners.

Wired for Books. This Web site features audio discussion of Carver's work by professors Marilyn Atlas and Edgar Whan and also includes a follow-up session in which Whan and Atlas answer questions posted to the Web site by e-mail. (http://www.tcom.ohiou.edu/books/)

CHARLES E. MAY

Willa Cather

BORN: December 7, 1873, Back Creek Valley, Virginia
DIED: April 24, 1947, New York, New York
IDENTIFICATION: Early twentieth-century writer of novels, short stories, poems, and nonfiction, considered one of the foremost interpreters of the American pioneer experience.

Although Willa Cather was born in Virginia, her family moved to Nebraska when she was just nine years old. There she encountered the rich cultural diversity and hard life of the early settlers in Nebraska. Her elegantly written and psychologically profound novels often deal with the problems that occur when different cultures live together. Her early major novels, such as *O Pioneers!* (1913) and *My Ántonia* (1918), examined life in Nebraska, but her later novels, such as *Death Comes for the Archbishop* (1927) and *Shadows on the Rock* (1931), explored how Europeans came to understand and appreciate the cultures of Native Americans and First Canadians.

The Writer's Life

Willa Cather was born on December 7, 1873 in the small farming community of Back Creek Valley, Virginia, near the city of Winchester. She was the first child of Charles and Mary Virginia Cather. Her given name was Wilella, but her family called her Willie. She later chose to go by the name of Willa, selecting Sibert as her middle name, in honor of her maternal grandmother, Rachel Sibert.

Childhood. Life in post-Civil War Virginia was difficult, and for this reason the Cathers joined Charles's brother and parents in Webster County, Nebraska, in 1883. There Cather continued her education and experienced at first hand the real difficulties that early farmers had in transforming the prairies of Nebraska into successful farms. Cather's parents farmed for just one year, after which they sold their farm and equipment and moved to Red Cloud, Nebraska, where Charles became a shopkeeper.

Most Nebraska farmers in the 1880s and 1890s were immigrants from many European countries, including Sweden, Norway, Germany, Russia, and France. The rich ethnic mix of these immigrant farmers first introduced Cather to other cultures and sparked her literary and creative imagination. In high school, Cather acted in amateur plays, studied Greek and Latin, and read widely in European literature.

Education. In 1890 Cather moved to Lincoln, Nebraska, and enrolled in a two-year preparatory school at the University of Nebraska. She graduated from the university in 1895. During her college years she wrote extensively on theater and literature for the two campus magazines and for the *Nebraska State Journal*, already displaying the impressive quality of her literary talents.

Journalism. After graduation, Cather worked briefly as a reporter for the *Lincoln Courier*, and in the following year she moved to Pittsburgh, Pennsylvania, where she lived for ten years. There she wrote short stories, reviewed plays and concerts for Pittsburgh news-

Cather's life typifies the American experience. Both her story and that of her family are one of immigration, movement, and change. Her family traces its ancestry to Ireland, from where they emigrated in the 1750s, eventually settling in Pennsylvania. The date of this photograph is unknown.

papers and magazines, and taught Latin and English in Pittsburgh high schools.

In 1905 she published her first collection of short stories, *The Troll Garden*. This book contains her most famous short story, "Paul's Case," which describes with great insight the psychological problems of a profoundly depressed teenage boy. Cather's story illustrates the destructive nature of clinical depression, which, with early intervention, can be treated successfully.

Cather accepted a job as a staff writer at *McClure's* magazine and moved permanently to New York City in 1906. Within two years she was made managing editor of the magazine. In 1912, she met the influential American author Sarah Orne Jewett, who recognized Cather's literary talent and persuaded her that working at *McClure's* was preventing her from becoming a successful writer. Cather stopped working as a journalist and editor in 1912, concentrating solely on writing and leading a relatively quiet life. She had several close friends, including Isabelle McClung, Edith Lewis, Dorothy Canfield Fisher, and Elizabeth Shepley Sargeant, but her main activity was writing.

A cover of the June 1898 issue of *The Home Monthly*. Cather served as managing editor of the magazine from July 1896 to June 1897, but she gave up the post as she grew to dislike the domestic, pedestrian nature of the publication.

The Home Monthly office (left) was located in the section of Pittsburgh known as East Liberty. The date of this photograph is unknown.

Early Success. Between 1912 and 1918, Cather produced three masterpieces in which the principal character in each novel is a strong woman who maintains her independence despite attempts by men to control her life and limit her freedom. *O Pioneers!* and *My Ántonia* both take place in her beloved Nebraska. These two novels reveal an exquisite style and deep understanding of the human condition. They remain her most popular works and are regularly studied in high school and college English classes. Cather's 1915 novel *The Song of the Lark* describes the artistic and intellectual development of a young singer named Thea Kronborg.

Cather's first novels were praised by noted critics such as H. L. Mencken and Edmund Wilson for their fresh voice, and Cather herself enjoyed early and enduring literary and economic success. Throughout the 1920s, Cather continued to write and to expand her understanding of other cultures. She did not rely solely on secondary sources but instead traveled to places that interested her. Her extended stays in the American Southwest, where she learned at first hand about Native American cultures, greatly informed her novel *Death Comes for the Archbishop*. In 1928 she went to Quebec City, where she came to appreciate the culture and history of Quebec, which became the subject of her next novel, *Shadows on the Rock*.

Although *Death Comes for the Archbishop* and *Shadows on the Rock* were enormously successful with the American reading public, critics' reviews were somewhat muted in their praise. Many American critics were uninterested in, or unsympathetic to, Cather's explorations of cultural encounters between whites and Native Americans in *The Professor's House* (1925) and *Death Comes for the Archbishop* and between French colonists and First Canadians in *Shadows on the Rock*. Such response denies the true depth of these three novels.

Although American critics reacted rather unfavorably to *Shadows on the Rock*, both French- and English-speaking Canadians quickly accepted it as an extraordinary masterpiece and the greatest novel in

Thomas Eakins's 1881 oil painting *The Pathetic Song* (Corcoran Gallery of Art, Washington, D.C.) echoes the independent spirit of Thea Kronberg, the singer in Cather's 1915 novel, *The Song of the Lark*. Cather became known for her portrayal of strong, multifaceted female characters, many of whom encounter difficulty relating to a society that expects women to be dependent on others.

This portrait of Cather was taken between 1906 and 1912, the years she spent as a writer and editor for *McClure's* magazine in New York.

FILMS BASED ON CATHER STORIES

1924	*A Lost Lady*
1934	*A Lost Lady*
1980	*Paul's Case*
1991	*O Pioneers!* (TV)
1992	*O Pioneers!* (TV)
1994	*Spring Awakening* (TV)
1995	*My Ántonia* (TV)

English on the French colonial experience in Canada. This initial Canadian assessment did not change after the novel's original publication in 1931.

Awards and Honors. Cather had the good fortune to be considered among the most admired American novelists during her lifetime; she received many prestigious literary awards for her work. In 1923 she was awarded the Pulitzer Prize for her novel *One of Ours* (1922). She won the Howells Medal, awarded for fiction by the American Academy of Arts and Letters, in 1930; the Prix Féminin Américain in

1933 for her Quebec novel *Shadows on the Rock*; and the Gold Medal in 1944 from the National Institute of Arts and Letters.

Later Years. Throughout the last two decades of her life, Cather remained a prolific writer, completing several important novels, including *Lucy Gayheart* (1935) and *Sapphira and the Slave Girl* (1940); a collection of essays entitled *Not Under Forty* (1936); and a posthumously published collection of short stories, *The Old Beauty and Others* (1948). Cather died of a cerebral hemorrhage on April 24, 1947, in New York City. In accordance with her wishes, she was buried in Jaffrey, New Hampshire, a town she had visited several times between 1918 and 1938 that had given her the inner peace she needed to write creatively.

HIGHLIGHTS IN CATHER'S LIFE

1873	Willa Cather is born on December 7 in Back Creek Valley, Virginia.
1883	Moves with her family to a farm in Webster County, Nebraska.
1884	Moves with her family to the town of Red Cloud, Nebraska.
1890	Graduates from high school in Red Cloud; begins studies at the University of Nebraska in Lincoln.
1895	Graduates from the University of Nebraska.
1896	Moves to Pittsburgh, Pennsylvania, where she lives for the next ten years, writing stories and reviews for local magazines and newspapers and teaching Latin and English in high schools.
1905	Publishes her first collection of short stories, *The Troll Garden*.
1906	Moves to New York City to work as a staff writer for *McClure's* magazine.
1912	Meets Sarah Orne Jewett; leaves *McClure's*; publishes her first novel, *Alexander's Bridge*.
1913	Publishes *O Pioneers!*.
1915	Publishes *The Song of the Lark*; visits New Mexico.
1918	Publishes *My Ántonia*.
1920	Publishes short story collection, *Youth and the Bright Medusa*.
1923	Receives the Pulitzer Prize for *One of Ours*; publishes *A Lost Lady*.
1925	Publishes *The Professor's House*; spends the summer in New Mexico.
1927	Publishes *Death Comes for the Archbishop*, set in New Mexico.
1928	Visits Quebec City; begins writing *Shadows on the Rock*, set in Quebec City.
1930	Receives the Howells Medal for fiction from American Academy of Arts and Letters.
1931	Publishes *Shadows on the Rock*.
1932	Publishes a short-story collection, *Obscure Destinies*.
1933	Receives the Prix Féminin Américain for *Shadows on the Rock*.
1935	Publishes *Lucy Gayheart*.
1936	Publishes a book of essays, *Not Under Forty*.
1940	Publishes *Sapphira and the Slave Girl*, her only novel set in Virginia.
1944	Receives Gold Medal from the National Institute of Arts and Letters.
1947	Dies of a cerebral hemorrhage on April 24 in New York City; was buried in Jaffrey, New Hampshire.
1948	Her short-story collection *The Old Beauty and Others* is published posthumously.

The Writer's Work

Despite the great diversity of settings and themes in Willa Cather's short stories and novels, there is a unity in her work. Even during her student days at the University of Nebraska, the writing in her published essays and reviews was of the highest quality. It is largely for this reason that she had little difficulty finding work with magazines and newspapers in Nebraska, Pittsburgh, and New York City.

Issues in Cather's Fiction.

Cather always wrote clearly, but her magazine articles often dealt with ephemeral topics. A few years after her arrival in Pittsburgh, she began writing short stories that explored such serious topics as death and dying. In early stories such as "A Death in the Desert" (1903) and "Paul's Case" (1905), she helps her readers to see the world through the eyes of people who are suffering and dying. Even in these early works, she revealed a deep understanding of human psychology and the problems of ordinary people with whom her readers can easily identify.

People in Cather's Fiction.

Cather's major characters tend to live on the margins of society. In "Paul's Case," for example, the main character is a clinically depressed teenager who cries out for help, but no adult intervenes to save his life.

In "A Death in the Desert," Katharine Gaylord is a musician who once performed works composed by the famous but exceedingly vain composer Adriance Hilgarde. As Hilgarde's brother, Everett, is traveling through Wyoming, he is asked to visit Katharine, who is dying on a distant farm. Everett stays with her for weeks and helps this woman, whom he barely knows, to die peacefully. Cather illustrates that Everett and Katharine, who have led relatively obscure lives, are more sensitive and morally better people than the renowned composer Adriance Hilgarde.

The Theme of Women and Outsiders.

An important theme in Cather's work is that of the emotionally strong woman who overcomes difficult situations, inhospitable climates, and, especially, antagonism from insensitive men who try unsuccessfully to control her. With quiet dignity, intelligence, and inner strength, Alexandra Bergson, the eldest of the four children and the only daughter of John Bergson in *O Pioneers!*, displays vision and a willingness to take risks. Her daring enables her family to escape poverty and to become relatively wealthy. Her accomplishments are even more impressive when it is considered that she is constantly belittled by her brothers Lou and Oscar, who have benefited from her sound financial decisions.

Equally strong and independent women characters can be found in the singer Thea Kronborg of *The Song of the Lark* and in *My Ántonia*'s Ántonia Shimerda, a simple and hardworking woman of Bohemian descent who succeeds in the harsh environment of

Cather once wrote, "When I strike the open plains, something happens. I'm home. I breathe differently. That love of great spaces, of rolling open country like the sea—it's the great passion of my life."

Imogene See's *Nebraska Farmstead* (Museum of Nebraska Art in Kearney, Nebraska) presents the typical sod structure many pioneers called home. As there was little wood to be found on the mostly treeless plains, settlers built their houses from blocks of earth that were held together by the grasses' thick network of roots. Cather greatly admired the resourceful spirit of the pioneers.

SOME INSPIRATIONS BEHIND CATHER'S WORK

Nebraska despite her difficult childhood as an indentured servant and her lack of a formal education. Although Ántonia's life is difficult, she remains a profoundly happy woman, sharing her joy of life with others.

In some of Cather's later novels, the emotionally strong character is not a woman but is still someone who lives on the margins of society. In *Death Comes for the Archbishop*, the principal character is a French missionary of refined taste named Jean Marie Latour. To Latour's great surprise, he is named the bishop of a diocese that covers New Mexico, Arizona, and even Colorado. With determination and a strong commitment to improving the spiritual lives of the Mexicans, Euro-Americans, and Native Americans in his huge diocese, he replaces complacent and morally corrupt priests with honest missionaries.

Near the end of his long life, Bishop Latour has an opportunity to return to a very comfortable life in his native France, but he

Willa Cather read voraciously as a child, and her short stories and novels contain numerous references to the classic and modern literature she absorbed. The most important influences on her work were her own experiences during her adolescent years on the plains of Nebraska and during her research trips in the American Southwest and Quebec, which enabled her to understand other cultures from within these cultures. She was the first major American writer to try to understand cultures in which many American intellectuals of her era were not interested. Navajo and Quebec cultures were generally not appreciated by Americans during Cather's lifetime, but she helped her readers to understand the universal values other cultures can teach those who set aside preconceived ideas.

chooses instead to stay with his people in New Mexico. His decision parallels that of the French missionaries in *Shadows on the Rock*, who take permanent vows to remain in the equally harsh environment of Quebec in order to serve the spiritual needs of French colonists and First Canadians. Cather's interest in the dignity of common and often extremely poor people displeased certain elitist critics, who lamented her choice of subjects, such as cliff dwellers in *The Professor's House* and *Death Comes for the Archbishop* and poor merchants in *Shadows on the Rock*.

Cather's Literary Legacy. The incredible beauty of Cather's prose style continues to bring real pleasure to her readers long after her death. Her well-crafted sentences and para-graphs prompted a *Time* magazine journalist to suggest that "Willa Cather could not possibly write a bad novel." Cather's exquisite prose style enabled her readers to experience for themselves the rich psychological complexity of her major characters, who never descend to the level of those who attempt to belittle them. They have such strong inner strength that they willingly forgive those who caused them great suffering.

In *Death Comes for the Archbishop*, Bishop Latour sends his friend Father Vaillant to hear the dying confession of an excommunicated priest named Father Lucero, who had scandalized the Native Americans in his parish with his morally unacceptable behavior. Through his willingness to forgive Father Lucero, Bishop Latour saves him from eternity in hell.

Cather's 1931 novel, *Shadows on the Rock,* examines the lives of the French-speaking settlers of seventeenth-century Quebec who eked out a living amidst the sprawling Canadian wilderness. The above illustration by an unknown artist depicts the challenges faced by early Canadian settlers. This art appeared in the publication *Canadian Scenery Illustrated, 1842.*

In *O Pioneers!*, Alexandra Bergson goes to a prison in far-away Lincoln to talk with and to console the man who killed her beloved brother, Emil.

In her twelve novels and in many of her short stories, Cather described how different cultures can coexist despite true cultural misunderstanding. In her major Nebraska novels, such as *O Pioneers!* and *My Ántonia*, she effectively contrasts the conflicts between Scandinavian and French immigrants in Nebraska farming communities. When her brothers Lou and Oscar treat her in an especially insensitive manner, Alexandra Bergson stops going to the Lutheran church of her youth and starts attending the local French Catholic church because its priest and parishioners meet her spiritual needs.

In *Death Comes for the Archbishop*, the cultural encounter is among Navajos, French missionaries such as Bishop Latour and Father Vaillant, and Euro-American settlers. They all learn to live together in their new community. Bishop Latour meets the spiritual needs of all members of his diocese, but he also helps the Navajos and the Euro-American settlers to respect each other's cultures. A similar situation occurs in *Shadows on the Rock* in which the French colonists and First Canadians gradually learn to live together in the new society of Quebec that they are creating together.

BIBLIOGRAPHY

Arnold, Marilyn. *Willa Cather's Short Fiction*. Athens: Ohio University Press, 1984.

Gerber, Philip. *Willa Cather*. Boston: Twayne Publishers, 1975.

Lee, Hermione. *Willa Cather: A Life Saved Up*. London: Virago, 1989.

McFarland, Dorothy. *Willa Cather*. New York: Frederick Ungar, 1972.

Middleton, Jo Ann. *Willa Cather's Modernism: A Study of Style and Technique*. Rutherford, N.J.: Fairleigh Dickinson University Press, 1990.

O'Brien, Sharon. *Willa Cather: The Emerging Voice*. New York: Oxford University Press, 1987.

Sergeant, Elizabeth. *Willa Cather: A Memoir*. Lincoln: University of Nebraska Press, 1963.

Urgo, Joseph R. *Willa Cather and the Myth of American Migration*. Urbana: University of Illinois Press, 1995.

Wagenknecht, Edward. *Willa Cather*. New York: Continuum, 1994.

Woodress, James. *Willa Cather: A Literary Life*. Lincoln: University of Nebraska Press, 1987.

LONG FICTION

1912 Alexander's Bridge
1913 O Pioneers!
1915 The Song of the Lark
1918 My Ántonia
1922 One of Ours
1923 A Lost Lady
1925 The Professor's House
1926 My Mortal Enemy
1927 Death Comes for the Archbishop
1931 Shadows on the Rock
1935 Lucy Gayheart
1940 Sapphira and the Slave Girl

SHORT FICTION

1905 The Troll Garden
1920 Youth and the Bright Medusa
1932 Obscure Destinies
1948 The Old Beauty and Others
1965 Willa Cather's Collected Short Fiction, 1892-1912
1973 Uncle Valentine and Other Stories: Willa Cather's Collected Short Fiction, 1915-1929

POETRY

1903 April Twilights

NONFICTION

1936 Not Under Forty
1949 Willa Cather on Writing
1956 Willa Cather in Europe
1966 The Kingdom of Art: Willa Cather's First Principles and Critical Statements, 1893-1896
1970 The World and the Parish: Willa Cather's Articles and Reviews, 1893-1902 (2 vols.)

MISCELLANEOUS

1950 Writings from Willa Cather's Campus Years

Reader's Guide to Major Works

DEATH COMES FOR THE ARCHBISHOP

Genre: Novel
Subgenre: Historical fiction
Published: New York, 1927
Time period: 1848 to the 1880s
Setting: New Mexico

Themes and Issues. At first glance, *Death Comes for the Archbishop* seems very different from Willa Cather's best-known novel, *O Pioneers!*. *Death Comes for the Archbishop* takes place not in Nebraska, but in New Mexico, and the major character in this novel is not a woman, but a French Catholic priest named Jean Marie Latour. There are, however, several links between *Death Comes for the Archbishop* and *O Pioneers!*.

In both novels, French Catholic immigrants are significant characters. The principal characters of both novels, Bishop Latour and Alexandra Bergson, learn to appreciate the values of a different culture. Both must overcome adversity and inhospitable climates.

While writing *O Pioneers!*, Cather relied on her own experiences growing up in a multicultural community in Nebraska. In her preliminary research for *Death Comes for the Archbishop*, she made three extensive trips to

This 1919 oil painting of a New Mexico landscape by Marsden Hartley reflects the varied landscape of the Southwest that Cather found so appealing. Always expanding her horizons, Cather embarked on a tour of the Southwest in 1912. The Anasazi cliff dwellings she saw there fascinated her.

Arizona and New Mexico to learn about the co-existence of Navajo, Mexican, and Euro-American cultures in areas acquired by the United States after the Mexican War.

The Plot. The story begins in 1848 when the pope appoints Jean Marie Latour, a French missionary, as the bishop of the newly created diocese of Santa Fe, New Mexico. Father Latour, a well-educated Frenchman, is unaccustomed to extremely hot weather. He and his assistant and friend, Father Joseph Vaillant, make a hazardous trip to New Mexico. When he and Father Vaillant reach Santa Fe, they are one of the few truly committed priests in this diocese. Father Latour does encounter a blind priest whose spirituality and care for his parishioners impress the bishop very much. The local priests refuse to accept Father Latour as their new bishop, fearing that he will force them to end their profligate lifestyles. Father Latour must travel alone to Mexico to receive his official appointment certificate.

After his return to Santa Fe, Latour is finally accepted as the new bishop but must also deal with several serious issues. He comes to appreciate Navajo and Mexican cultures. He travels to distant parts of the diocese to serve the spiritual needs of the Navajos, who have been neglected by Mexican priests. When two corrupt and influential priests, Father Martinez and Father Lucero, who exploit their parishioners and openly violate their vows of chastity and poverty, refuse to obey Bishop Latour's orders, he excommunicates them.

Bishop Latour cares deeply about the needs of ordinary people in his huge diocese and refuses to yield to corruption. He makes judicious use of episcopal authority to persuade the American rulers of these newly acquired territories to treat Navajos with more respect.

Slowly Bishop Latour brings other missionaries to his new diocese and begins training

Francois Marius Granet's oil painting *Priest at the Altar* (Musee des Beaux-Arts, Caen, France) reflects the commitment and forbearance resident in Bishop Latour, the devoted missionary in Cather's *Death Comes for the Archbishop*. Unlike some of the other priests in the diocese, Latour turns his back on worldly concerns and temptations.

young men from the diocese for the priesthood. He leads an exemplary life, building schools and churches throughout his diocese and spending time meeting the spiritual needs of Catholics in his diocese, which later becomes an archdiocese.

Because he travels everywhere on a simple mule, readers understand that Bishop Latour is a humble man truly committed to serving God and his community. He is always willing to stress the accomplishments of others. After his retirement as bishop, he has the opportunity to return to a comfortable life in France, but he realizes that his people still need his spiritual guidance in Santa Fe and chooses to remain there.

Analysis. The novel Cather considered her finest, *Death Comes for the Archbishop*, celebrates the life of a simple man who, like her Nebraskan pioneers, struggles to settle the American frontier. Cather's love for the Southwest is evident throughout her richly detailed and thoroughly researched novel that brings to life a chapter in American history.

SOURCES FOR FURTHER STUDY

Dollar, J. Gerard. "Desert Landscapes and the 'Male Gaze': *Death Comes to the Archbishop*." *Willa Cather Pioneer Memorial Newsletter* 42, no. 1 (Summer 1998): 6–9.

Skaggs, Merrill M. "Willa Cather's *Death Comes for the Archbishop* and William Faulkner's *The Sound and the Fury*." *Faulkner Journal* 13, nos. 1–2 (Fall 1997–Spring 1998): 89–99.

Woodress, James. "*Death Comes for the Archbishop*." In *Willa Cather: A Literary Life*. Lincoln: University of Nebraska Press, 1987.

O PIONEERS!

Genre: Novel
Subgenre: Regional realism
Published: Boston, 1913
Time period: 1880–1900
Setting: Webster County, Nebraska

Themes and Issues. Six of Cather's twelve novels and many of her short stories take place in Nebraska, where she came of age. Her early experience of the harsh life and the rich cultural diversity of the early Nebraska settlers served to inspire many of her most important works, which she wrote years later in distant states such as Pennsylvania, New York, and New Hampshire. She frequently wrote lyrically of her incredible love of the open prairies of Nebraska, and her eloquent style successfully conveyed the aesthetic pleasures of the landscape.

O Pioneers! established Cather as one of the most important American novelists of the twentieth century, and the many short stories and novels that she wrote before her death in 1947 solidified this reputation. Many critics consider Cather, along with William Faulkner, one of the most profound and creative American novelists of the twentieth century.

The Plot. *O Pioneers!* is a third-person narrative of the struggles of Scandinavian and French settlers on the plains of Nebraska over a twenty-year period from the 1880s until the first decade of the twentieth century. It is as well a narrative of the intellectual and moral development of its strong female protagonist, Alexandra Bergson. The Bergsons and their four children have emigrated from Sweden in the hope of finding a better life.

As the novel begins, the adolescent Alexandra has come to town to purchase medicine for her dying father, John. Readers quickly realize that John will not live very long. He places his full trust in Alexandra, his eldest child and only daughter, to preserve and manage their farm and to look out for her mother and three brothers, Lou, Oscar, and Emil. Emil is only five years old when his father dies, and he remains Alexandra's favorite brother.

The two older brothers, Lou and Oscar, are disorganized and intolerant. They shy away from taking risks and rely upon their sister to bring them financial success, but they do not respect her abilities and achievements. The fact that Alexandra is a strong and independent woman intimidates Oscar and Lou.

Because her late father loved the land so much, Alexandra is unwilling to sell the fam-

Helen Lundeberg's 1934 oil painting *Pioneers of the West* (Smithsonian American Art Museum, Washington, D.C.) offers a glimpse of Cather's beloved Nebraska plains, where the sweeping miles of grass would suddenly resolve into chalky, almost lunar landscapes.

ily farm. For several years after John Bergson's death, his children are successful as farmers, but then a lengthy drought persuades many people to sell their farms. During the middle of this drought, Alexandra and Emil visit several farms in the surrounding valley, selecting appropriate land to purchase. Despite harsh criticism from Oscar and Lou, Alexandra mortgages the family farm in order to purchase other farms as investments. She is convinced that the value of land will increase significantly and then she will be able to sell some of the land for a large profit, ensuring both a comfortable lifestyle for the four Bergson children and a proper education for Emil.

Oscar and Lou believe that farmers can make money solely by growing crops. Their sister Alexandra, however, is a visionary who competes with the bankers and businessmen who purchase farms as investments. At the time when the novel takes place, financial investment was a field largely dominated by men. Ironically, Alexandra succeeds where her brothers Oscar and Lou would have failed. She alone takes the risk of signing the mortgage pa-

The woman in Frank W. Benson's 1909 oil painting *Sunlight* (Indianapolis Museum of Art, Indianapolis, Indiana) mirrors the independence of Alexandra Bergson, the heroine of Cather's *O Pioneers!* Alexandra, a woman with keen foresight, always kept her eyes firmly planted on the future.

pers so that she can buy more land. Despite the protests of Oscar and Lou, Alexandra goes ahead with her investment.

At this point many years pass before the story resumes. Alexandra's financial success has enabled her to give farms to both Oscar and Lou and to share with them their part of the original investment. She has also paid for Emil's education at the University of Nebraska, Lincoln, where Cather herself studied from 1890 to 1895. Oscar and Lou have criticized Alexandra's spending her money on a college education, and they are especially displeased when Emil returns to their community and feels more comfortable with neighboring French Catholics than with Scandinavian Lutherans. Both Alexandra and Emil enjoy the company of the French Catholic immigrants who, in their opinion, are livelier and more open-minded than their Scandinavian friends.

Oscar and Lou permanently alienate Alexandra when they criticize her old friend Carl Linstrum, who returns to their village after sixteen years and whom Alexandra loves and plans to marry. Oscar and Lou are extremely rude and condescending toward their sister, treating her with contempt because she is a successful businesswoman. They persuade their neighbors not to welcome Carl into their community. The members of her own Lutheran church turn against Alexandra, and Carl concludes that he has no real choice but to leave Nebraska.

Alexandra maintains her dignity and independence. In refusing to be controlled by men, she illustrates the growing independence of women, who will no longer allow men to mistreat them. Cather mentions several times that Alexandra likes to read the Swedish Bible that had belonged to her late father. She remains very religious, but after Oscar and Lou prevent her marriage to Carl, she stops attending the Lutheran church and starts attending Mass at the local Catholic church. Although she does not go so far as to convert to Catholicism, she finds inner peace with her new Catholic friends.

After he graduates from the University of Nebraska, Emil returns home to the farm and becomes involved with a married French Catholic woman named Marie. Although it is suggested that the relationship is purely platonic, Marie's enraged husband, Frank, shoots and kills both Emil and Marie.

Alexandra, mourning the loss of her beloved Emil, travels alone to Lincoln for two reasons. She first wants to see if she can find students who remembered Emil, but she meets only freshmen who never knew him. Then she visits the prison where Frank is being held and speaks with him. She forgives Frank and even prays for him. After Emil's death, Carl returns to Alexandra's village. Alexandra and Carl share a love for each other and for the land. As the novel ends, it is clear that they will marry in order to end the loneliness that each feels apart from the other.

Analysis. Since its publication in 1913, *O Pioneers!* has been praised for the exquisite beauty of its prose style. The novel explores many important themes, such as alienation, cultural misunderstandings among different ethnic and religious groups, and the liberation of women from male dominance. Alexandra Bergson demands and obtains the dignity and respect that she has earned.

SOURCES FOR FURTHER STUDY

Frus, Phyllis, and Stanley Corkin. "Willa Cather's Pioneer Novels and (Not New, Not Old) Historical Readings." *College Literature* 26, no. 2 (Spring 1999): 36–58.

Paniccia-Carde, Mary. "Creative Fertility and National Romance in Willa Cather's *O Pioneers!* and *My Ántonia.*" *Modern Fiction Studies* 45, no. 2 (Summer 1999): 275–302.

Urgo, Joseph R. *Willa Cather and the Myth of American Migration.* Urbana: University of Illinois Press, 1997.

Wagenknecht, Edward. "Novels: Studies in Fulfillment." In *Willa Cather.* New York: Continuum, 1994.

Other Works

"PAUL'S CASE" (1905). Although Willa Cather owes her literary fame largely to her profound and beautifully written novels, she also wrote many fine short stories, which are frequently anthologized. Her best-known short story is "Paul's Case," originally published in her short-story collection *The Troll Garden*. "Paul's Case" deals with the topic of adolescent suicide. Despite its third-person narration, the story intimately conveys Paul's desire to end his life. At the same time it relates Paul's strange actions, which are clearly unanswered cries for help.

As the story begins, Paul is facing a disciplinary committee at his high school in Pittsburgh. Cather once taught English and Latin in Pittsburgh high schools, and she was familiar with the psychological problems of adolescents. Paul's antagonistic attitude toward his teachers makes him unpopular with them. Although the teachers and the principal vote to suspend Paul from school, the perceptive drawing teacher senses that something is wrong with Paul, seeing not a happy teenager but rather a hopeless old man. The teachers, however, make no effort to refer Paul to a competent psychologist for the help he desperately needs. Not even Paul's parents take much notice of his violent mood swings and difficulty in sleeping, attributing them to the normal difficulties of adolescence.

Paul enjoys attending theaters and concert halls less because he is fond of plays and classical music, but more because he likes the artificiality of plays and operas. The beautifully dressed actors and opera singers allow him to imagine that he can escape the drab conditions of his home and neighborhood. He desperately seeks a way to escape everyday reality in Pittsburgh.

When he is asked by his employer to carry two thousand dollars to a local bank, he steals the money and travels to New York City. There he buys elegant clothes and checks into an expensive hotel in Manhattan. He lives in a world of illusion for one week, but his depression deepens as the stolen money runs out.

The young man in George Tooker's 1949 tempera-on-panel painting *Cornice* echoes the desperation of Paul in Cather's best-known short story, "Paul's Case." Cather's firsthand knowledge of the charged emotional life of teenagers gave "Paul's Case" the ring of authenticity.

He purchases Pittsburgh newspapers and learns that the theft has been discovered, but that his father reimbursed his employer, who has agreed not to press charges against Paul. Paul's father travels to New York City to save his son, but Paul throws himself in front of a train before his father finds him. Paul has second thoughts as the train approaches, because he recognizes too late "what he had left undone."

Resources

In her will written in 1943, Willa Cather designated her friend Edith Lewis as her executor and trustee of her estate. She asked that Lewis destroy all manuscripts and letters in her possession and prevent film adaptations of her books. Lewis carried out Cather's wishes; as a result no manuscripts of Cather's novels and short stories now exist. Lewis lived until 1972, when Cather's nieces and nephews then inherited the rights to her works. They and their heirs permitted some films to be made from her books, and her works have been included in anthologies.

No one library possesses a strong collection of Cather's letters. Letters written by Cather to her publishers at Knopf and Houghton Mifflin and to friends and family members can be found in numerous libraries throughout the United States. In addition to the Cather Archive in Red Cloud, Nebraska, other libraries and archives that possess important Cather documents are the University of Texas Library in Austin, the Nebraska State Historical Society in Lincoln, the University of Nebraska Library in Lincoln, the Morgan Library in New York City, Yale's Beinecke Rare Book Library, and the Huntington Library in San Marino, California. Other sources of interest for students of Willa Cather include the following:

Willa Cather Pioneer Memorial Foundation. This organization was created in Red Cloud, Nebraska, in 1955 to preserve and manage sites in Webster County, Nebraska, important in Cather's life and fiction. This organization publishes a quarterly journal entitled *Willa Cather Pioneer Memorial Newsletter*, which includes information on Cather historic sites and articles on her works and is the only scholarly journal on Willa Cather. This foundation also has an important Cather archive, which is open to the public. (http://www.willacather.org)

The Cather Garden of the University of Nebraska-Lincoln Botanical Garden and Arboretum. This garden, on the university campus in the state that influenced much of Cather's writing, pays tribute to the prairie landscape. The brochure to the garden prints biographical information about Cather and her inspirations for her writing. (http://www.unl.edu/unlbga/tour/cather.html)

Willa Cather Page. This Web site contains a list of publications pertaining to Cather, a list of events featuring Cather's work, biographical information, quotations, and links. (http://icg.harvard.edu/~cather/)

EDMUND J. CAMPION

Index

Page numbers in **boldface** type indicate article titles. Page numbers in *italic* type indicate illustrations.